STUDIES
IN
PROVERBS

....

Wise Words in a
Wicked World

STUDIES IN PROVERBS

Wise Words in a Wicked World

Charles W. Turner

BAKER BOOK HOUSE
Grand Rapids, Michigan

ISBN: 0-8010-8815-1

Third printing, March 1985

PHOTOLITHOPRINTED BY CUSHING - MALLOY, INC.
ANN ARBOR, MICHIGAN, UNITED STATES OF AMERICA

Table of Contents

I. Getting Acquainted with Proverbs 11

II. Knowledge, a Firm Foundation 21

III. Wisdom Always Wins 31

IV. Work, Money and Stewardship 41

V. Words That Wound . . . Smiles That Heal 51

VI. Six Things God Hates—No, Make It Seven 61

VII. Small, But Smart 71

VIII. A Father and Son Chat 81

IX. The Truly Liberated Woman 91

X. Running Rascals and Bold Lions
. . . Guilt vs Righteousness 101

XI. Proverbs Regarding Life's Problems 111

XII. Social Problems Are Always with Us 121

XIII. In Conclusion 131

TO

JUNE AND JEFF

Who have made our house a home!

Acknowledgments

How do you thank fellow workers for being helpful? Not by words alone I am certain, but until I find a better way this will have to do. There have been many kind friends who have taught me by their presence the lessons of life I trust you will find in this book. They have reflected God's reality in their lives which has made mine such a pleasant one. They have contributed more than they will ever know.

Introduction

Purpose of This Study

There must be two things in the heart of any author before he begins a manuscript. One is he must feel a reason to write—an opinion that he has something to say. The other is there must be someone to whom he wants to communicate. Both of these thoughts were significant to me because for some time I had been experiencing a love affair with the Proverbs. When it all started I am not certain, but I do know when it came to full bloom. Asked to teach the literary values of the Bible to a class in the high school at Rittman, Ohio, the Book of Proverbs came to my mind. The instruction was to be for just two sessions—an hour each time. In preparation for this, I read and reread the Proverbs as never before. They came to life and spoke to me as God's truth. The appeal of these strong, short, true-to-life phrases made me laugh and cry. They made me see the practical side of truth and left me with a feeling of challenge as well as a sense of failure in my own life. Here I found truth in street clothes and found a need to apply knowledge in a fresh new way called wisdom.

Some years have passed, but I never really considered translating my love affair into writing. The opportunity was never there, nor was the desire; but when the opportunity did come, I wanted to use it. The desire to stimulate a practical, warm-working, Christian experience helped me to decide to try to put into words the thoughts which I had found in

Proverbs. My desire is to relate these words so that everyone can understand them—the young as well as the old. I did not set out to bring forth a literary gem, and I have no illusion about this ever happening. But I hope I can impart to you some of the joy I have found in my study.

I speak and share with all of those wonderful people who work in factories, fix cars, drive trucks, teach school, sit long hours in the office and then all come together to worship and study on Sunday mornings. I write to all who have added so much to my life by being honest and open, who did not always agree with me, but who added a dimension to my life. This book is to communicate to them—not in the language of a scholar but in the fellowship of a warm heart.

How do you treat Proverbs? How do you outline the book? The topics run so much together that they separate only to come back into a common stream. At times it seems to cut back and forth across the road of thought much like one of those little twisting rivers or streams you see along the highway. I have sought to reflect on some of the oft-repeated topics of Proverbs, yet have touched but a few. We will deal with units of thought rather than sections and outlines that break the book into segments. Proverbs is just like life—a single day is like a single chapter. In each there is included many varied incidents and happenings to challenge our thoughts.

Where are we going? We are going to learn a lesson about life and about wisdom. When it is all over I trust you will see God is real and that He wants to live in your world because it really is not yours—it is His.

Winona Lake, Indiana
September, 1975

I.

....

Getting Acquainted
with Proverbs

THE CHAPTER OUTLINED:

  I. **What Is a Proverb?**

      A. Proverbs Are Plentiful

      B. Proverbs Make Plain . . . Sometimes

  II. **The Book of Proverbs—When and Who?**

      A. The Historical Setting and Biblical Placement

      B. The Author of Proverbs

  III. **The Purpose of Proverbs**

      A. Instruction and Training

      B. Understanding or Insight

      C. Wise Dealings

      D. Shrewdness and Discretion

      E. Knowledge and Learning

SUGGESTED DAILY DEVOTIONAL READING

Monday—A Proverb of Parenthood (Jer. 31:27-30)

Tuesday—Physician Heal Thyself (Luke 4:21-30)

Wednesday—Understanding of Proverbs (John 16:25-33)

Thursday—One Choice—You Name It (I Kings 3:5-15)

Friday—Wisdom Put to the Test (I Kings 3:16-28)

Saturday—The Wisest Man in the World (I Kings 4:29-34)

Sunday—Reasons for Reading the Bible (II Tim. 3:12-17)

As a preface to our study in the Book of Proverbs, it will be well for us to spend a little time in getting acquainted. This is a whole new area of exploration for most people, and I am certain you will find it a delight. As is true of all new acquaintanceships, it takes more than a formal introduction to make a new friend, but that is where the procedure should begin. Most people have spent their Bible-study hours in the New Testament with such fascinating books as John, Romans, Corinthians, and the Pastoral Epistles. Readings in the Old Testament have been limited to Genesis and possibly the Psalms. Proverbs is not equated, in some Christians' minds, as the most desirable portion of the Scriptures and thus it is neglected. This neglect can result in missing hours of needful instruction and untold blessings. We trust your neglect will have terminated and you will find the sweet secrets of this part of God's honeycomb to be good spiritual nourishment.

I. WHAT IS A PROVERB?

A. Proverbs are plentiful. Proverbs have been found in almost every known civilization. In ancient times they literally abounded in the countries that surrounded Palestine. For example, in Egypt, Persia and Greece there were volumes of these wise sayings. They were not totally unique to Israel at all. One of the more famous of the books of proverbs was the Egyptian work, *Teaching of Amenemope.* In fact, the writings of Solomon in Proverbs and the Egyptian works were so close together at times that much discussion has resulted in seeking to find which was first. During the past few years more and more scholars have moved to the position that it has to be the Egyptians borrowing from the Hebrews and their writings. It is our position that this is true, but for now we are seeking merely to point out the existence of proverbs.

In the entire Old Testament one should notice that proverbs abound. They were used by prophets, but there were also other men of wisdom. Let us look at several examples of proverbs which may not have appeared to be such in your previous contacts. In a conversation between David and Saul in a very tense situation in their relationship it was David who came forth with a proverb taken from the ancients. If you will turn to I Samuel 24:13-14 you will find David quoting the following proverb: "Wickedness proceedeth from the wicked." Another illustration of a proverb is Jeremiah 31:29-30—"The fathers have eaten a sour grape, and the children's teeth are set on edge." Yet another use of the proverb is found in I Samuel 10:11-12 when it became a popular saying—"Is Saul also among the prophets?"

When we come to the New Testament, we find that Christ used many proverbs, for example: "Physician, heal thyself" (Luke 4:23). The expression was a familiar one and thus He used it to present a timely message to the people. Paul used a proverb that was well known when he said: "The Cretians are always liars, evil beasts, slow bellies" (Titus 1:12). So we find proverbs are plentiful in each age and society.

What about today? Proverbs, anyone? "An apple a day keeps the doctor away," is always a good opener. What about a "Stitch in time saves nine"? "Rome was not built in a day," is often quoted as a friendly reminder to those who think everything should happen overnight. How many can you bring to mind of the much-used proverbs of your locale when you were growing up? The Pennsylvania Dutch folks have a great variety of them, and there are many well-known Chinese proverbs, and so it goes. The point I wish to establish is that proverbs have been evident in all groups of society.

B. Proverbs make plain . . . sometimes. Proverbs have been defined in various ways. Most often they are classed as pithy sayings or comparisons or as brief sayings that set forth practical wisdom. Oftentimes they appear in poetic form as we find them in the Book of Proverbs. They are generally the result of mankind's observations that have conveniently been set forth in a brief conclusion. They could be generally called the conclusion and evaluation of a total situation. The "gem" of truth that forgets the details and leaves you with the sum and substance of the whole matter. Let me illustrate a proverb of early America. Benjamin Franklin was a man of great thrift and concern about material things. He observed at great length the methods and manners of the care of money. One of the proverbs attributed to him is: "A penny saved is a penny earned." This is a conclusion to the matter of work and the benefits that can be retained. In other words, you must save it before it is really yours.

Proverbs, while being an observation and conclusion to known information, could also be expanded in meaning and use. Such an illustration is Proverbs 17:3 and Malachi 3:3. The basis for the statement in Malachi was taken from the conclusion of the proverb in the 17th chapter with new meat added to the bones of the truth.

Proverbs are at times very clear in their meanings, but this is not always true. Sometimes they turn out to be very difficult to comprehend. Then they become dark sayings. A very interesting illustration of this is found in the final days of the ministry of Jesus Christ. John 16:25 and 29 tell us that the disciples could not always understand the proverbs or the parables that Jesus used in His teaching. So proverbs make plain . . . but not always. Certain truths can be obtained by those who desire it. However, truth does not come quickly or easily if our desires do not function.

It might be well at this point to make at least a comment on the difference between a parable and a proverb. This line cannot always be clearly drawn, but for our practical approach of study, let us make a few distinctions. A parable is generally longer than a proverb and is more extended as far as detail is concerned and often seems to be presented in a narrative form. The proverb is usually short and has a definite conclusion or moral within the presentation. Having said this, I am aware that sections of Proverbs have narrative forms, such as the section we shall study about the father's advice to the son. So beware of seeking to draw the line too sharply between these two forms.

The Book of Proverbs comes to us by way of revelation, but in other realms man can speak wisely within a specific area of knowledge, without any special revelation from God. We also know that proverbs have been presented in just about every area of life; for instance, in connection with money, industry, politics, home and family—to name only a few. Proverbs are used to tell what the weather will be tomorrow or what it will be like months ahead. A proverb can find a home in almost any setting. All it needs is a wise man with an observant eye and a way with words.

II. THE BOOK OF PROVERBS – WHEN AND WHO?

When it comes to a background study of any book of the Bible, people are sometimes hesitant to get excited. This is a natural aversion that some have to the study of history. But an accurate background is essential to the understanding of any event. The time and place are essentials.

A. The historical setting and Biblical placement. There are three books in the Old Testament called the Wisdom Books. They are Job, Proverbs and Ecclesiastes. They follow the historical section of the Old Testament and are grouped with such poetic books as Psalms and Song of Solomon. The writing of the Book of Proverbs by Solomon, which we will discuss a little later, helps to identify the historical period. It comes during the period of the kings of Israel and places us in the 8th or 9th century before Christ. A time when Israel was back in the Land of Promise after their experiences in the country of Egypt. This was when great glory was coming to the people and the country was in the process of building.

The placement of this book in the canon was made on the basis of the content and type of writing rather than on the chronological setting. The writing of Job, for instance, was probably in a much earlier period of Jewish history.

B. The author of Proverbs. Solomon is generally admitted to be the author of a major share of the book. The mention of Azur and King Lemuel in chapters 30 and 31 seems to indicate their authorship of the last two chapters of the book. It has been argued these are other names for Solomon. Some have argued for an editorship of portions of the book with the gathering of the material sometime after the death of Solomon. This conclusion is based on the statement of Proverbs 25:1 where reference is made to King Hezekiah who lived some 250 years after Solomon. We will, however, assume the authorship of the book to be Solomon and present some credentials and illustrations showing his great wisdom and ability.

Solomon, the son of David, was a great man in many respects. The material apex of Israel's history can be traced to the events of this man's reign. The temple built under the direction of the king sets forth the majesty and beauty of his interests. But Solomon was noted for another mark of prominence and greatness and it was his wisdom. I Kings 3:5-28 tells of the beginning of Solomon's reign and his meeting with God. His humble heart asked one thing of the Lord and that was for "an understanding heart to judge thy people, that I may discern between good and bad: for who is able to judge this thy so great a people?" (I Kings 3:9). The response of the Lord is found in verse 11 where it is recorded that God is pleased that Solomon did not ask for long life, riches for himself, nor for the lives of his enemies; but rather understanding. The wisdom obtained from God by Solomon is made clear in verse 12, "Behold, I have done according to thy words: lo, I have given thee a wise and an understanding heart; so that there was none like thee before thee, neither after thee shall any arise like unto thee."

Immediately Solomon is put to a test regarding his wisdom as he must make a decision between two women as to whom the one child belongs (I Kings 3:16-28). The word soon spread to the people of Israel that indeed a wise man ruled over them (v. 28).

Further qualifications for the writing of this book are set forth in I Kings 4:29-34 where we learn God's gift of wisdom was so great there was no one like Solomon in the east country or Egypt. His fame spread through the nations, and people came to hear and see this man. He spoke three thousand proverbs and he wrote five thousand and five songs. His knowledge was of trees (botany), beasts (zoology), and verse 34 seems to cap the renown of this wise man.

This is the author of the book we are about to study. A man endowed with special wisdom from the Lord. Wise men had been known before, but none could compare with Solomon. God was with him in a special way and was to use him to write the Book of Proverbs.

III. THE PURPOSE OF PROVERBS

Having established some background facts about the book and its author in a general historical setting, let us for a brief period endeavor to ask why we are studying the material. Derek Kidner in his study on Proverbs sets forth facets of wisdom which he says "all shade into one another, and any one of them can be used to represent the whole." I would like to use them to point out the reasons for studying this book and place an explanation with each to guide us. There will be a close resemblance here to II Timothy 3:16 as to the purposes of the Word of God.

A. Instruction and training (Prov. 1:2-3). Call it correction or reproof and it can all be summed up in discipline. Where there is the truth of the Scripture there is always the rebuke to our fallen natures. There is no other way than this. Before we can walk straight we have to change our way of walking. We must be instructed with truth and trained to obey, then we can be a disciple of the Lord. Here is a basic—a foundation and a cornerstone. We can start building here and no other place.

B. Understanding or insight (Prov. 1:2; 2:2). Let us give it another name, "common sense"; or, if you come from the right part of the country, it is "horse sense." In a study of the Bible, and of this section in particular, you will notice references to the word "understanding," which is an ability to strip aside the obvious and come to the heart and core of the matter very quickly. So often people spend their time on the outskirts of a problem and never seem to be able to come to grips with the situation. Paul prays for the believers in Ephesians that they "may be able to comprehend [understand] with all saints" (Eph. 3:18). Our study in Proverbs will help us get to the very heart of the matter in many of the important moral and spiritual issues of our time.

C. Wise dealings (Prov. 1:3). This deals with practical wisdom and has to do with action or involvement. Could we inject the terms "heart knowledge" and "head knowledge" at this point? So many can get their doctrines straight, but they have trouble with the fruit of the Spirit. Their systematic theology stands in straight lines and jotted tittles, but their ability to cope with crises in everyday life has gone wrong. Herein lies the beauty of true wisdom—it works Monday through Friday with amazing efficiency.

D. Shrewdness and discretion (Prov. 1:4). We fear the word "shrewd" which is considered in a bad light to mean a low level of scheming. In the positive, and good sense, it arises to the level of the ability and power of projecting plans (cf. Prov. 22:3). The truth tells you where you are going and how to get there. So many Christians do not endeavor to make plans in the will of the Lord. The person without goals and direction will not be a leader, because he himself does not have his face set towards the "mark." Another of the purposes in the study of the Book of Proverbs is to gain a proper direction, which in some cases is *toward* an object or goal and in other cases it is to *turn away* from the crisis or situation.

E. Knowledge and learning (Prov. 1:5). Our last group of words speaks to us of the authority of truth. Knowledge finds its source in God but flows to us as an active stream to motivate not merely our minds but our wills. The whole man is eventually touched by truth. He grasps through his mental processes, he is motivated to exercise his will in compliance, and feels the blessings of this surrender and motivation of truth. Here is the whole spectrum of knowledge and learning that affects the whole man.

So the purpose of our study is to let you know knowledge (mind); exercise wisdom (will); and feel truth (emotion). Proverbs will make a new person out of you; because if you are willing, God can work through this portion of Scripture just as He intended it to work. Join with us on a venture through some new land, one of spiritual excitement on a practical level. If you will permit it, you will be touched by humor as you see man living in a real world—just like the one you are in right now. You will come out a better person than when you started, because that is the way God works.

DISCUSSION QUESTIONS

1. Proverbs are a part of every culture. Can you decide what makes a proverb a proverb? What is the difference between a proverb and a cliché?

2. Why do you suppose Christ used some proverbs that were not clear to His listeners?

3. Discuss the relationship between the proverbs Solomon wrote and the special wisdom he received from God. How is this wisdom reflected in the book?

4. What are the similarities between II Timothy 3:16 and Proverbs 1:2-5?

II.
....

Knowledge, a
Firm Foundation

THE CHAPTER OUTLINED:

  I. Knowledge Begins with a Fear of God
    A. Definition of Knowledge
    B. Acceptance of Knowledge
    C. Channels of Knowledge

  II. Knowledge Rejected Brings Disaster
    A. Fools Reject Instruction
    B. Cost of Rejection

  III. Knowledge Received Demands Diligence
    A. Opposition to Receiving Truth
    B. Diligent Pursuit of Knowledge

SUGGESTED BACKGROUND DEVOTIONAL READING

Monday—The Way of Blessing (Prov. 3:5-10)
Tuesday—His Ways and Our Ways (Isa. 55:7-13)
Wednesday—Channels of Knowledge (Ps. 19:1-14)
Thursday—Follow Christ (John 10:1-5)
Friday—The Cost of Knowing (Prov. 1:28-32)
Saturday—How Foolish Can You Get? (Ps. 14:1-7)
Sunday—Crumbling Foundations (Matt. 7:24-29)

Throughout the Bible there is a constant discussion of knowledge. It may appear under such words as truth, understanding, and so on; but the meaning is the same. We are to *know* God, to *know* the truth, and even to *know* ourselves. There is an earnest desire expressed by one of the writers of the Word when he stated, "I would not have you to be ignorant" (I Cor. 10:1). Ignorance is the other face of knowledge—it is the negative aspect. As darkness is the absence of light so ignorance is absence of truth and knowledge.

Jesus claimed to be "the truth" (John 14:6). He is full knowledge in person (incarnation). Men have sought knowledge throughout history only to miss it when they failed to take God into their lives. And no man is truly knowledgeable until the light of truth reaches him from the Light of Truth—God.

No knowledge of history can be complete without accepting Biblical truths. No psychologist can discern deeds of man until he knows God. No teacher can stand to proclaim facts without the light of truth. The world and the people in it remain a mystery until all are unlocked by the revelation of the Bible.

I. KNOWLEDGE BEGINS WITH A FEAR OF GOD (Prov. 1:7; 3:5-6)

A. Definition of knowledge. Throughout our study in the Book of Proverbs we will note two words that appear repeatedly. They are *knowledge* and *wisdom*. We shall make a distinction in the two. *Knowledge* will be defined as basic fact and truth. It is information that is accurate and dependable. We shall use the word *wisdom* as the use of facts in a practical way. A man may learn and gather information and truth, but it is not until this truth is put into action on a practical level that it becomes wisdom. This is true in the spiritual sense as well as in all other areas.

Send two persons to an instructor. Both will be taught the same set of facts. This is the gathering of knowledge. For an illustration let us suppose that two men have been instructed in how to organize and operate a business. Now comes the test. One man will become a success and the other a failure, or at least one will do much better in his area of responsibility than the other. Why? Because one will take the knowledge and through wisdom translate it into the actual operation of the business. He will sell his product, buy materials wisely, and not let his overhead run away from him. He will advertise with skill. He becomes a financial success. The other person spends each day going over the notes from the instructor (the basic set of knowledge), but he cannot transfer the information into practice.

Now let us see if our distinction will carry over into the spiritual realm. You can tell two people about God. One of them will take this knowledge and ask Christ to come into his heart as Saviour. The other person will retain in his head the knowledge of how to be saved, but it never reaches his heart and will. (Knowledge, but the absence of wisdom). This is what we commonly call heart and head knowledge in a non-technical definition of Christian experience.

B. Acceptance of knowledge (v. 7). Let's begin with true knowledge. The word *true* is not necessary, but let's use it for emphasis. If it is not true knowledge, it is really not knowledge. Like the Gospel, there is not *another* gospel, there is only one.

If a man is to find truth and knowledge he must begin with God. The writer of Proverbs expressed it this way in verse 7: "The fear of the Lord is the beginning of knowledge." The word "fear" is best defined in chapter 3, verse 5—"Trust in the Lord." If we are to find out what full truth is we must make a complete commitment to God. This involves the rejection of our own understanding (3:5). After all, our ways are not His ways (14:12). An acknowledgment of Him will result in having His direction (3:6). Note the closeness of acknowledge to knowledge.

As we mentioned in the opening of this chapter, the only

basis of understanding in this world is to have the knowledge of God. There is no consistent explanation of this world, or of man and what is going on around him without a knowledge of God. It is in the Book. And when a person is willing to trust the Lord in and for all things, and has a fear of God, then, and only then, is there a beginning of knowledge. Each one must become as a little child if he desires to grow in knowledge.

C. **Channels of knowledge.** God is the beginning of knowledge, and He has chosen to reveal His knowledge to us through various channels. We will but mention them here because time will not permit their full discussion. The key to the channel of knowledge is instruction, and this word is repeated constantly in the Book of Proverbs. Instruction is given through the following channels:

1. The Bible—Psalm 119
2. Creation—Psalm 19:1-6
3. Christ—Colossians 2:9; Hebrews 1:2
4. Prophets—Hebrews 1:1
5. Pastor-teachers—Ephesians 4:11

II. KNOWLEDGE REJECTED BRINGS DISASTER (Prov. 1:24-33)

From the previous section we have found the importance of knowledge and its source. Mankind, having the power of choice, has been offered the privilege of trusting God and entering into full knowledge. But as with all matters with an offer, there is always the option of rejection. This is the warning of the writer of Proverbs. The warning is pertinent and relevant because more people reject God's offer than accept it. The majority is on the broad way that leads to destruction, while the minority finds the straight road that leads to life.

A. **Fools reject instruction (v. 7).** A fool is the opposite of a wise man. A fool is a fool because he rejects knowledge and therefore is void of it. The complete fool is mentioned in Psalm 14:1. He says, "There is no God." Compare this statement with Proverbs 1:7. "The fear of the Lord is the beginning of knowledge."

Here we have the extremes of what this subject is all about. When you remove God, you remove knowledge because He is not only the source of it, He is IT. There is no greater fool in all the world than the rejector of God. It matters not the number of degrees behind the name, nor the position he may hold, for without God the person is without fact.

B. Cost of rejection (vv. 24-33). The key to this passage is verses 24 and 29: "Because I have called, and ye have refused . . . they hated knowledge."

1. *Fear and desolation will come (v. 27).* We have put forth knowledge as the firm foundation. When it is refused, there is no foundation at all. When the time of trouble comes, fear is followed by destruction. Christ is the foundation according to Paul's instruction to the Corinthians (I Cor. 3:11). When a person's life is built upon God, the ability is given to withstand and meet the whirlwind. The building will remain standing even after the test of judgment has come.

Christ presented the most graphic picture of certain foundations. The illustration is so simple and beautiful that a chorus for children has been written about it. It deals with the wise man and the foolish man. The one builds on the rock and the other builds on the sand. The test comes and the one survives and the other fails. The account is in Matthew 7:24-29. Thus, there is a warning that the foundation determines the end results.

2. *Knowledge rejected leaves a vacuum to be filled (vv. 30-31).* A man who will not have God in his life will eventually turn to something else. Generally this person fills the void himself. God rejected—man accepted. He will "eat of the fruit of . . . [his] own way." This fruit will prove to be bitter.

There are a number of classic examples in the Scripture showing mankind rejecting the truth. When this takes place, the man has some form of idolatry. If the unseen God is rejected, man then will turn to the things he can see. Absence of faith demands replacement of sight. God's way versus man's way—not a very even contest. Isaiah tells of this voyage into idolatry (40:18-31). The contrast between God and idols is pictured in this passage.

It is left to Paul in the writings to the Romans to show the ultimate trip from God to total disaster. Moving from rejection of the invisible God, from thankfulness, to a proclamation of human wisdom the path trends downward through idolatry, moral lust, and degeneration. The end of the line comes after all forms of unrighteousness have been transversed. The person stands at the judgment (Rom. 1:20-32).

3. *The end of rejected knowledge (Rev. 20:11-15).* The high cost of nonacceptance of truth is not only a wasted life, but it is also a wasted eternity. The result of rejected truth is best set forth in a statement by Jesus Christ (cf. John 3:17-20). Condemnation comes when belief in Christ is not exercised. Remember, "trust in the Lord" is a commandment found from one end of the Bible to the other. We find it in the Old Testament as well as the New. To reject this command is to be confronted with the final judgment.

The White Throne is the final act of judgment on the part of God. Those who are not saved are there, and they are sent into eternity to be forever separated from the presence of God. In our common communication we address this as hell. This term encompasses the ultimate cost of rejected knowledge.

III. KNOWLEDGE RECEIVED DEMANDS DILIGENCE (Prov. 2:3-6)

Granted, there are many channels of knowledge flowing to people, and it is God's desire that all of us receive the blessings. Nevertheless, there is opposition to our receiving it.

A. Opposition to receiving truth. There is one who stands in the way of all people obtaining and using knowledge and that is Satan. As God is the Father of truth, so is the devil the author of lies. He will oppose and confuse in every way possible to keep people from achieving a knowledge of God. So it is not easy to overcome the opposition, and it is impossible to do it in the strength of the flesh. The power of God must come into action to be victorious in this phase of our life. If Satan can keep individuals from Christ, he will. But he sometimes settles by keeping a Christian weak in Biblical truth, and thus ineffective.

Human nature is not concerned about seeking after truth. It is basically selfish and degenerate. To follow God involves self-denial and rejection. This is not the way of the "old man." After we are saved, there is still the tendency to submit to the influence of the old nature. To yield to self rather than the Holy Spirit who dwells in the believer is a constant problem.

B. Diligent pursuit of knowledge (2:3-6). Two words in this passage demonstrate the need of seeking after truth: "*criest* after knowledge" (v. 3) and "*seekest* her" (v. 4). Both of these words are strong action verbs. To get knowledge one must really want it. In life we must have a firm desire, and this desire must be joined with a resolve of will to reach out for the things we want.

Life is composed of a number of decisions. These choices are made in a framework of time. We all have a limited amount of this commodity. Thus somewhere in our lifetime we decide what we want, and what we plan to obtain. This may not be a formal decision written out on paper, but nevertheless it is real. We spend our time doing what we consider most important to us in reaching our goals.

Christians need knowledge, but they must realize there is opposition to obtaining it. Now the question is—how much do we want it? Check your life and you will find the answer.

27

It is very easy to say the right things according to Christian doctrine, but it is another matter to do them.

Our writer of Proverbs says we should seek God and His truth with the same spirit and zeal as the man who seeks silver or a hidden treasure (v. 4). If God's people would practice such devotion, our churches would be revolutionized.

As a youth I lived with the stories of men seeking hidden treasures, and somehow hoped I could discover a buried box of coins or some precious jewelry. Men will spend a fortune already attained to find a treasure yet hidden. The allusion of great riches robs them of the riches already in their possession. Remember the dog who stood on the bridge with a bone in his mouth? And as he looked in the water below he saw his own reflection, but to him the dog below had a bigger bone. He dropped the bone in his own mouth to grasp the other. He ended with nothing!

We, as believers, should be ashamed of our lack of spiritual zeal when we see the zeal of those who seek material wealth. In like manner we should be diligent in giving out the knowledge of God with the aid of the Spirit. Truth does not come with great ease, but the rewards to the seeker are unlimited (2:6-9).

Another good lesson in "knock, seek and find" is diligence in prayer. This instruction is cited by Christ in Matthew 7:7. The point being that all of God's blessings are not falling equally in the lives of all His people. Yes, the blessings are there ready to fall, but the determination of the seekers varies.

REFLECTING—God is truth and is the source of it. Knowledge begins when we trust Him. Since God is truth, to reject Him is a disaster for time and eternity. The person who finds truth will do so with some degree of opposition. It is available through many channels as it comes into the range of our experience; but to be a real victor, one must desire it enough to seek it.

DISCUSSION QUESTIONS

1. What is the difference between knowledge and wisdom?

2. How has God chosen to reveal truth to mankind? Do His methods change with time?

3. What is the value of truth to man for this age? For eternity?

4. Why is the pursuit of truth often so difficult, while lies come so easily?

III.

....

Wisdom
Always Wins

THE CHAPTER OUTLINED:

   I. **Wisdom Defined**
   A. From the Dictionary
   B. From the Bible

   II. **Wisdom Obtained**
   A. The Source of Wisdom
   B. The Receiving of Wisdom
   C. Some Examples of Biblical Wisdom

   III. **Wisdom and Its Rewards**
   A. The Reward of Happiness
   B. The Reward of True Values
   C. The Reward of a Long Life
   D. The Reward of a Good Night's Sleep

   IV. **Wisdom, the Prime Priority**
   A. Wisdom, the Principle Thing
   B. Wisdom in Its Ultimate Sense

SUGGESTED BACKGROUND DEVOTIONAL READING

Monday—A Wise Man Is a Happy Man (Prov. 3:13-19)

Tuesday—Wisdom Is for the Asking (James 1:1-9)

Wednesday—The Principle Thing (Prov. 4:1-9)

Thursday—Stephen, the First Deacon (Acts 6:1-8)

Friday—Combined Talents Build a Tabernacle (Exod. 36:1-8)

Saturday—A Wise Man Wins Souls (Prov. 11:25-31)

Sunday—Wise Men Walk by Faith (Heb. 11:6-16)

Having completed our study on the subject of knowledge as the firm foundation, it is now time to deal with the twin sister of knowledge—wisdom. We have found the great need of building a proper and solid foundation under our lives. Without the personal knowledge of God and a trust in the Lord, any life is doomed to complete failure. Once the foundation of Jesus Christ is established it is time to build upon it. An important building block of this spiritual life is the wisdom that comes from God. We want to look at the subject of wisdom from four different aspects. We want to define it, we want to know how to find it, we want to know its rewards, and, finally, we want to put to use the ultimate wisdom.

I. WISDOM DEFINED

A. From the dictionary. This source is not always the best place to ascertain the meaning of spiritual truth; nevertheless, the dictionary can be of help in finding the basic meaning of words. Webster tells us that wisdom is the "ability to judge soundly and to deal sagaciously with facts, especially, as they relate to life and conduct." We would add that the word "sagaciously" means "to be keen in discernment." Other words that carry a similar meaning to wisdom are: sane, prudent, sensible, sage with understanding and discernment.

Thus we conclude that wisdom can be ascribed to a person who possesses the ability to understand the ends to be reached and the means of achieving those ends. In other words, one who is able to apply facts to life and conduct. The truly wise man is sane, prudent, sensible and sage. He knows how to live his life and how to apply principles to everyday situations which will produce the very best results and accomplishments.

B. From the Bible. When we turn to the Scriptures we find wisdom applied to the extension of knowledge as it relates to everyday activities. I find many applications of the relationship of knowledge to wisdom in the Bible. It presents knowledge as the basic truth and wisdom as that truth in action. Several illustrations to this would be the mentioning of these two words such as is found in Proverbs 1:4, 7; 2:6. These are but a few examples of where knowledge and wisdom appear in the same context.

We see in these examples that the Bible is filled with illustrations of wisdom, and the Book of Proverbs is part of the "wisdom literature" of the Old Testament. Two other books that deal with wisdom literature are Job and Ecclesiastes. In God's Word a person who could perform well in his particular area of skills such as a hunter or one skilled in carving is called wise. When Moses set about to construct the tabernacle he chose several wise men. Their names were Bezaleel and Aholiab. If you read Exodus 35:30-35 you will find the Spirit of God filled them and with this came wisdom, understanding and knowledge. Their wisdom rested in all manner of workmanship and crafts to complete the tabernacle and thus do the work of the Lord. They were able to put knowledge into action and do God's will.

Note another example of wisdom as cited concerning David in II Samuel 14:20. Here David's ability to judge and to know is called "the wisdom of an angel of God." You do not have to be a king to be wise—the craftsmen and builders had it also. Neither do you have to be a missionary nor a minister to have it. Remember it was bestowed on such a man as Job.

II. WISDOM OBTAINED (Prov. 2:6; James 1:5)

A. **The source of wisdom** (Prov. 2:6). Before you try to obtain an object it is best to determine its source or where it can be found. If you desire food, you go to the grocery store where it is sold. If you want clothing, you go to the retailer who handles this type of merchandise. When it comes to wisdom, the Bible makes it very clear where the source is to be found. It is in God. Proverbs 2:6 states, "the Lord giveth wisdom." If knowledge comes from God it only stands to reason that the implementation of knowledge would also come from Him. There is a warning in Proverbs 3:7 that we are not to be wise in our own eyes. This appears to put us on guard against taking God's truth or knowledge and misapplying it for our own purposes.

B. Receiving wisdom. If God gives wisdom, then the next question is how can a person get it? According to James 1:5 you and I are to ask for it. We must sense a need for wisdom first of all. This is where the lack comes into the picture of our lives. When we are deficient in this area and realize our need, we are then to ask from God. There is a promise in this verse that He will supply you with an abundant degree of wisdom for the asking. This along with other promises of the Bible, should be used in the glorifying of God through the usage of that which is obtained. One of the prayers of our daily devotions should be for the wisdom of God in each hour of our lives. Christians pray for so many other things, but how many pray for daily wisdom? Could it be we fill our heads with knowledge and then do not know what to do with it? There are many knowledgeable Christians, but there are lamentably fewer wise Christians. God, please give us more commonsense Christians who know how to live and to communicate to us on our level of existence.

C. Examples of wisdom given (Acts 6:1-4). There appears to be a number of examples in the Scriptures of wisdom being given without the person involved asking for it. We have already noted the case of God supplying wisdom to the men who built the tabernacle. Another important example is found in the early days of the church. As the church grew so did the misunderstandings and problems. The Greeks and the Hebrews had a problem concerning the care of the widows. The Greeks felt their widows were being neglected; therefore there was a need to settle the issue and have men appointed to see that justice and equity were followed. The qualifications are outlined in Acts 6:3. They were to be "men of honest report, full of the Holy Ghost and *wisdom*"—honest, spiritual and with the ability to settle the problems of people in disagreement. What the Early Church needed, the church of the present could well use in abundance; that is, deacons with wisdom to help meet the needs in today's church.

III. WISDOM AND ITS REWARDS (Prov. 3:13-26)

A. The reward of happiness (v. 13). "Happy is the man that findeth wisdom" is the opening comment in this section on wisdom. Happy and blessed are two words used throughout the Bible in an interchangeable way. The word "blessed" to the modern man conveys little. It is a word removed from the present-day understanding. Ask somebody about being blessed and you get a vague stare. Ask him if he wants to be happy, and you have struck a responsive chord in his thinking.

A person will not be completely happy until he becomes wise. The opposite of a wise man is a foolish man. When a person is not wise and does not know how to make his daily life function properly, he is going contrary to God's will. Sorrow will be his lot. Happy is the wise person who applies truth to his daily duties and serves God wisely.

B. The reward of true values (vv. 14-15). To decide the true values of life is not easy. In fact, the process of just making a decision is seldom easy. From the moment you arise in the morning until you go to sleep at night, your life is one continuing series of decisions. The wise person will make the right decisions: the foolish person will make the wrong ones. Wisdom is better than the merchandise of silver or the gain of gold or the preciousness of rubies. Remember this was written several thousand years ago. The very items of wealth mentioned by Solomon are the very things considered precious in our day. The price of gold has soared as has silver.

Gold and silver coins are precious today. Rubies, who could buy them? But wisdom is better than them all.

Yes, wisdom is better than silver, gold or rubies. Having said this we are conscious this is not the decision of most men. Many have placed a higher premium on the material objects than they have on the intangible substance of wisdom. The true values of life are what we should seek, and wisdom is the truest of the true. The reward of wisdom is greater than the rewards of gold. The need is to be wise enough to choose wisdom over wealth.

C. The reward of a long life (vv. 16-18). The promise of length of days is not foreign to the Bible. You will find it in connection with the giving of the Law and obedience to it (Exod. 20:12). Then in the New Testament there is a reference by the Apostle Paul of the length of days being associated with honor to parents (Eph. 6:1-3). We do not hear a great deal of preaching on this subject. I am not certain of the reason for this neglect, but the promise is in the Word of God to those who will follow the instructions.

One of the rewards of wisdom is not only the length of life, but the quality of life. The wise man's ways are pleasant and peaceful. Wisdom is a tree of life to them that lay hold upon her. So the wise man will have many days and they will be good days. The great virtue of the length of days is that they will be filled with good things. However, the life filled with wickedness and lack of wisdom has very little value.

D. The reward of a good night's sleep (vv. 21-26). Has it occurred to you that one of the rewards of the wise man includes a good night's sleep? Wisdom is better than Sominex and this I can prove by the words of Solomon. Read them and believe them. "When thou liest down, thou shalt not be afraid: yea, thou shalt lie down, and thy sleep shall be sweet" (v. 24).

Are you beginning to see that wisdom pervades all of life and it is so practical that it is beyond our human understanding. This is one of the problems of most Christians—they are still living separated lives. They separate the knowledge they possess from a Monday through Saturday experience. Wisdom is the connecting force between our Bibles and our hearts. Ask for wisdom and receive the rewards. They are practical and down to earth, and this is where you are presently living.

IV. WISDOM, THE PRIME PRIORITY (Prov. 4:7-9)

In this chapter we have sought to define wisdom. Then we discussed its source as being from God with prayer being the channel by which it is obtained. Its values and rewards have also been examined. We want to conclude this chapter with a strong appeal for you to place your priorities in proper order. Though we have touched on the subject already in this chapter, we desire to stress its importance even more.

A. Wisdom is the principle thing (v. 7). The discussion of wisdom continues throughout the Book of Proverbs. The sight of it is never lost. Several of the chapters bear down very hard on its importance. The reason should be rather obvious to all of us. The world has had need in every generation of people who can take knowledge and truth and communicate them. These are the wise people.

The church needs wise pastors, deacons, trustees, teachers and janitors. We could use some wise ushers and secretaries as well—people who can relate and are honest people of good report, filled with the Holy Ghost and wisdom. If we in the church would place a priority on wisdom and realize it is a possession of great worth, then we could really be involved about the business of bringing people to God and God to the people. Too often our Christian tasks have been foiled and stagnated by our inability to implement great truths. The power of the Gospel with its great truth has been chained in shackles instead of being unleashed on the world. We need wise persons who can lead us to the proper application of the

Bible. The church stands waiting to conquer; the truth is there, but the giant does not attack because it does not know how.

B. Wisdom in its ultimate sense (11:30). Who is the truly wise man? There may be many who would suggest an answer to this question. Certainly an answer is found in the Book of Proverbs—"... he that winneth souls is wise." This statement is irrevocable, is it not? There may be many ways to be a wise person, but none can deny the fact that a soul winner is near the top of the list. I think this statement should be placed in a wide context. The wise man influences people toward God and His will. This person knows God's truth and is desirous of seeing people come to the place of acceptance of this truth.

How do you influence others? There are a number of ways to do it. One sure method is through a godly life. Personal witnessing and clear teaching of the Scripture are certainly needful. The wise person not only applies all of the necessary truths to himself, but he makes it his responsibility to tell others. It will be wonderful to go to heaven. It will be even more delightful to take others with you as you go.

Only God can save a soul, but in His plan and providence He asks His children to share in the witness and the testimony. By His Spirit He convicts and convinces, then the hearer must make a choice of whether or not he wants to be saved. You can be wise if you will be the link in the chain of God's command by doing your part in getting the Gospel to the world.

REFLECTING—Wisdom always wins when it is God's wisdom working through the lives of His children. Wisdom is the application of truth and knowledge as revealed in the Bible. There are many blessings and rewards to the wise person and because of the importance of wisdom, we as God's people need to place a priority on obtaining it. Wisdom is available to all and it is from God. Be a winner—be a wise man.

DISCUSSION QUESTIONS

1. Give a definition of wisdom in your own words.

2. Since wisdom is available for the asking (James 1:5), why is it so often missing in the Christian's life?

3. Can wisdom be divided into categories of "sacred wisdom" and "secular wisdom"?

4. What are some of the rewards and benefits of wisdom?

IV.

Work, Money and Stewardship

THE CHAPTER OUTLINED:

    I. Work—The Action of Doing
        A. Positive Attitude Towards Honest Labor
        B. Negative Attitude Towards Honest Labor

    II. Money—The Reward of Doing
        A. Love of Money Is a Spiritual Problem
        B. Possession of Riches Is Not a Sin

    III. Stewardship—A Proper Use of Money
        A. Stewardship Is a Part of God's Plan
        B. Stewardship Results in Blessings

SUGGESTED BACKGROUND DEVOTIONAL READING

Monday—Lessons from an Ant (Prov. 6:6-11)
Tuesday—Contentment, a Basic Need (Prov. 30:1-9)
Wednesday—No Work—No Food (II Thess. 3:7-16)
Thursday—Dangers in Dollars (I Tim. 6:6-13)
Friday—Treatment of Others (Luke 6:27-38)
Saturday—Robbers in Church (Mal. 3:8-12)
Sunday—Happiness Is Giving (II Cor. 9:7-15)

When we come to a discussion of work, money and stewardship we have certainly moved into the realm of everyday living. In fact, the mention of work or money does not sound like topics to be discussed under a spiritual heading. But the Bible is filled with practical truth and instruction on these subjects. The purpose of this study is to deal with realistic aspects of life itself. So here we move into that area we call the Monday through Saturday part of our Christian lives. Then we will touch on—what many think of as the Sunday part—stewardship. But here again we will find it impossible to separate Christian living into days of the week. Our lives in Christ are really 24 hours a day and 7 days a week. They cannot be subdivided because it is Christ and us, and we are to live and work together in close fellowship. For failures, remember, we will have to take the blame . . . He is perfect!

I. WORK — THE ACTION OF DOING

Anyway we say it . . . work-vocation-labor-employment . . . it all comes out the same. It involves us and the time that we spend in making a living. Our place of employment tells people something about us, whether we are doctors, lawyers, salesmen, housewives or carpenters. It matters a great deal what we are because it is in this area where a great deal of our time and energy will be spent. Where and how we spend those 40 to 50 hours each week will have much effect on our Christian attitudes and growth. What we do can be good or bad on our testimonies. Let us look at several attitudes towards employment.

A. The positive attitude towards honest labor (6:6-8). We tend to divide our lives into the secular and the sacred. God does not make this same distinction. When a person goes to work in the morning as a believer, he is openly living his Christian life. What he does with this day will reflect his attitudes and basic philosophy. The writer of Proverbs shows us this truth.

1. *An example of industry—an ant.* The usual reaction of this illustration is . . . what can I learn from an ant? Well, there are at least two points here for emphasis. This insect does not need to have someone forcing her to work (v. 7). And next, apparently industry results in necessary provision for her and her own (v. 8). It is amazing what we can learn if we can keep our eyes and mind open to the happenings around us. But we tend to overlook the obvious and shut ourselves up from the best examples and illustrations of truth.

2. *Work without a supervisor (v. 7).* Let us look at the sheer industry of the ant. She has no guide, overseer or ruler. Can we put it into modern terms? She has no boss. I wonder how much work would be done in our modern era without an overseer or foreman putting gentle and sometimes not too gentle pressure on people moving them towards an intended goal. Whenever I see one of those signs along the roadway "MEN WORKING," I usually am disappointed, because I seldom see much action taking place. Men standing—yes; men talking—yes; but men working? Rare indeed.

The Apostle Paul in Ephesians 6 talks about the Christian and his attitude towards his employer. The term "servant" and "master" in the King James Version may seem a little stiff and harsh to the present-day employee, but the discussion has to do with working and laboring for another. Paul says, under the inspiration of the Spirit of God, that we are to obey our employers with a "singleness of heart." We are not to be clock-watchers (eyeservice), but we are to work as though we are doing the will of God. Show me a Christian with this attitude towards his employment, and I will show you a rare and a good person.

3. *Work provides for all seasons (v. 8).* The ant teaches us yet another lesson and this is "labor helps to provide for all seasons." Many do not "save for a rainy day" as was once a noble goal. Yet the Word teaches this is a good goal towards which we should strive. While in Egypt Joseph saved not for a

43

rainy day but a day when there was no rain. An entire empire was saved due to a dream from God. The days of plenty were followed by the days of little. Our dependence on welfare, on the union, and on many social organizations takes the sting out of the day of small income, but happy is the person who has learned the lesson of the ant. The Christian who fully provides for his own fulfills a spiritual function and to do so brings blessing. To fail is a spiritual disaster (I Tim. 5:8).

B. The negative attitude towards labor (6:9-11).

1. *The example of laziness*—"O sluggard." The ant stands for industry and the lazy one is exemplified in the term, sluggard. The word does not even sound good, does it? He is the person who will not face the responsibility of honest labor. His chief characteristic is sleep. Getting up in the morning is the most difficult thing most people do. Even with the beauty of music and a radio alarm there is nothing too great about getting up. Here the writer takes the negative attitude of people and associates it with sleep and laziness. Sleep is not a virtue when it comes to labor unless a man can find that rare job of being a "mattress tester," and I understand those openings are rare. Thus for the rest of us it is 8 hours a day in some other type of employment.

2. *Poverty and want will overtake the lazy man (v. 11).* Poverty is simply defined as doing without. You do not have what others possess who put forth honest labor. You may counter this thought by saying, yes, but this was written before the policies of social concern came to us. That is welfare, unemployment checks and so forth. I do not believe God's wisdom to man has been repealed. The person who will labor honestly as unto the will of God will reap many rewards not seen by the lazy man. The Psalmist said, ". . . yet have I not seen the righteous forsaken, nor his seed begging bread" (37:25).

Want will overtake the lazy man like an armed man. Want will come to the sluggard in its full thrust and overcome him. Need we define "want" for you? It is a desire for things. The slothful man will be possessed by the abundance of wants. The lazier he is the longer grows his list of wants. How dramatic is the statement of Paul when he says that the man who works not—eats not (cf. II Thess. 3:10). The results of not working brought about the urge of not to feed. Hunger can even help the lazy to see the value of work. Remember this sluggard is so named because of his attitude, not because of a physical problem. He is just plain lazy!

II. MONEY – THE REWARD OF DOING

Few things get more attention and greater criticism in Christian circles than does money. It is often damned in the sermon—just after the offering has been collected. If it is as evil as we sometimes proclaim, why is it sought after so diligently by the church itself? Obviously we misuse truth when it serves our own purposes.

A. Money loved is a spiritual problem (I Tim. 6:10). The spiritual problem with money, as in so many different areas of our lives, is the misplaced emphasis on it. It is the *love* of money that is the root of evil. When it is valued as so important that it becomes the goal and destiny in the life of the Christian, it can and does become a snare.

1. *A search for riches leads to temptation (I Tim. 6:9).* The main purpose of employment for most people is to gain money. This is a necessity because of the world in which we live. The utilities must be paid, the grocery must be visited, clothing must be purchased and so it goes. When the desire for wealth comes without proper role in relationship to God and need, then there is a valid temptation and snare. This is when we begin to trust in the tangible instead of God. The object that is seen is worshiped, and this is idolatry. We have discussed honest work and the providing for our needs as acceptable, but worship and trust in material things to bring fulfillment cannot be God's way.

2. *Misplaced emphasis on money can bring great sorrow (v. 10).* The key words in this verse are "love" and "coveted."

They express so strongly an attitude of the heart of the believer. When the Christian comes to this point in his life that money has become his love he has erred in his faith. The first and great commandment has been broken—"Thou shalt love the Lord thy God with all thy heart, and with all thy soul, and with all thy mind" (Matt. 22:37).

3. *Money cannot bring happiness (Luke 12:15).* Jesus explained that a man's life is not composed of the things he possesses. The amount of riches is not the true mark of success in the sight of God. Unfortunately, our modern society either marks a man by success or by failure on the basis of where he is in life and how much money he has. He has it made if he has a beautiful home and all of the funds needed to support this type of life. Yet the facts of experience and God's Word dramatically show us this is not true. Happiness in life is what a man is rather than what he has.

B. Possession of large sums of money is not evil. Many Christians get the mistaken idea that greed and love of money are only the traits of the rich. I think you will find an improper attitude and love of money present in the poor as well. In fact, those who do not have much must watch their attitudes because they may have a tendency to covet.

1. *Abraham was a man of wealth (Gen. 13:2).* A brief study of the life of Abraham will reveal his many possessions, and they were great by most any standard. Yet these riches did not prevent him from being an effective servant of God. He was a man who had spiritual problems, but they were not the direct result of his finances.

2. *Job is another example (Job 1:3).* In the first chapter of the Book of Job his material possessions are outlined clearly. Yet Job is declared to be a mature man in his faith in God. One of the attacks of Satan was to be towards these possessions. The test was to see if Job was serving God just because it was an easy way of life. When funds and family began to disappear, Job declared ". . . the Lord gave, and the Lord

hath taken away; blessed be the name of the Lord" (Job 1:21).

III. STEWARDSHIP – A PROPER USE OF MONEY

We have studied about work and its place in the Christian life, and then about money and the problem of its improper place in our lives. Now we must ask ourselves what we are to do with the fruit of our labors so that we will be in the will of God.

A. Stewardship of funds as part of God's will. For the time expended and the substance received, there is a need to realize that a portion of our possessions belong to God. Many Christians have learned the lessons of obedience in various areas of their lives, but find it difficult to learn the lessons of Christian giving. The Bible is filled with instructions on giving to the Lord, including the time of Abraham and his giving to Melchizedek a tithe and a tenth of the spoils (Gen. 14:20; Heb. 7:4). This giving of the tithe was prior to the institution of the Law. The tithe is the Lord's. God has always asked for a portion of the labors, and they are rightfully His already. The New Testament goes further than this and asks that the giving be as the Lord prospers (I Cor. 16:2).

1. *To hold back on God is robbery (Mal. 3:8-9).* The very thought of a church being robbed is a shocking thing to many people. Yet today many churches in metropolitan areas need constant protection even during the hours of worship. Offerings have been stolen from the front of the church during services. Worshipers have been held up and robbed. But Christians have been robbing God of His funds for centuries. Many show very little feeling of guilt about it. After all, they say they can hardly pay their bills with the 100 percent and could never make it with the 90 percent of their income. However, to withhold from God His tithes and offerings is to rob Him.

2. *Giving is an act of faith like other acts of obedience.*

47

Again we are faced with the problem of money being classified as secular and going to church being called spiritual. Witnessing for the Lord does not exempt you from all of God's other commands of obedience. We are not to pick and choose the orders of the Lord which we will obey. It is not like going to a store and deciding whether we want an orange or an apple or a plum. Doing God's will is accepting all of the commands.

When God commands us to give, we are to obey as an act of faith. Doing it because He told us, and then believing He will respond to fulfill His part. Faith is the act of an obedient heart that trusts God fully to know what is to be done. Sometimes we tend to go lightly on the teaching of Christian giving. If we do we are failing to help people grow to full maturity in all aspects of their Christian lives. Giving is an act of faith.

B. Stewardship in money brings rewards (Prov. 3:9-10; Mal. 3:10; Luke 6:38). There is a tendency to shrink back from emphasizing the rewards of a liberal heart in giving. It comes from a fear of a wrong motive of giving—people giving to get for themselves. While there can be a problem in this area, it is interesting to note God chose not to let it stand in His way of teaching blessings in giving. And we do not hesitate to use the principle of rewards in other areas of Christian incentives. Why are we so shy here? Possibly because we are still not too clear about the relation between money and our worship of God. The writer of Proverbs tells us to honor the Lord with our substance and the results will be barns filled and the winepresses overflowing. Not too much evidence of holding back a promise of reward, is there? It says we are to do our part and God will bless us! There might be some concern for many as to the motive of giving, but keep in mind the statement begins with: "Honour the Lord."

Malachi says much the same thing—stop robbing and start giving (Mal. 3:10). God asks the people to prove Him in the

48

matter of giving. Put Him to the test and see what happens. This requires faith and is a challenge from God. Meat in the house and a blessing too great to contain are the promises. You see, God gives rewards not only in the material realm but blessings for an obedient heart. There is no limit to the joy of an obedient heart even in the realm of money.

Yes, the passages mentioned above come from the Old Testament, but I understand it came from God the same as did the New Testament. Jesus talked to people about giving, and in Luke 6:38 He spoke of rewards both spiritual and material from so doing. Give and it will be given back to you. The returns are greater than the outgo. It will come back in good measure, pressed down, and running over. It is difficult to beat such a promise. No one else can make those kind of offers.

For further instruction on liberal giving go to II Corinthians, chapters 8 and 9. There Paul concludes the section by saying: "Thanks be unto God for his unspeakable gift" (9:15). If we are going to be like God we are going to have to learn to give like Him, because He is the greatest Giver and the greatest Gift.

REFLECTING—Honest labor is commanded and expected of a believer, and laziness is a sin that brings poverty. Money is evil when it becomes the love of the life and too much is expected of it. Faith in money and material objects is a subtle form of idolatry. Stewardship is expected and commanded, and it will bring rewards to the giver. The returned blessings are a happy heart of obedience, plus material increase.

DISCUSSION QUESTIONS

1. Is there a Christian work ethic? If so, what is it?

2. Can Christian principles be used at a secular job? Are they really effective?

3. Are money and possessions evil?

4. Is making a profit wrong? Is it sinful to profit from others?

5. What is a tithe? Should tithing be a standard for the modern-day church?

V.

....

Words That
Wound...
Smiles That Heal

THE CHAPTER OUTLINED:

I. Words That Wound
   A. Words Reveal Our Thoughts
   B. Words Cause Tensions and Trouble
   C. Words Feed Our Egos

II. Smiles That Heal
   A. A Friend Is a Helper
   B. A Happy Heart Is Good Medicine
   C. Kind Words Are Like Honey

SUGGESTED BACKGROUND DEVOTIONAL READING

Monday—Speaking from the Heart (Luke 6:39-45)
Tuesday—Untrustworthy Hearts (Jer. 17:5-10)
Wednesday—Tongues on Fire (James 3:1-18)
Thursday—A Cheerful Heart Is Good Medicine (Prov. 17:17-22)
Friday—Friendly People Make Friends (Prov. 18:19-24)
Saturday—Think Good Thoughts (Phil. 4:4-9)
Sunday—Strength for the Inner Man (Eph. 3:14-21)

Man was created as a social being and his basic nature bears out that fact. God had no sooner made a man than He created a helpmeet for him. In the normal pursuit of life we are in constant contact with other persons. Most of us consider a hermit's life as an abnormal existence. Learning how to live with each other and meeting the conflicts encountered will to a degree measure the depth of our Christian experience. Jesus said the second commandment is like unto the first, in that it deals with the subject of love. The first and great commandment speaks of our love to God and states that this love requires all of our heart and soul and mind. The second specification declares that we are to love our neighbors as ourselves (Matt. 22:34-40).

John, the apostle, spent much time in his epistles dealing with what we call interpersonal relationships. How we treat a brother is evidence of our spiritual condition. We cannot hate a brother without this attitude having an effect on our love for God. In this chapter we will take a look at several of the evident (external) reactions of one's heart condition—that is, speaking and smiling. We can either hurt or help others, and our spiritual state will determine which path we will walk.

I. WORDS THAT WOUND

A. **Words reveal our true thoughts (Prov. 23:7).** The Bible makes much use of the noun "word." In the first chapter of John, Jesus Christ is spoken of as the "Word." We call the Bible the Word of God. A word is a means of expression used to describe our thoughts and that which we desire to communicate to other people. The Lord Jesus Christ is the very expression of God and all the fullness of the Godhead is in Him bodily (cf. Col. 2:9). Moreover, the Bible is the expression of truth to mankind—it lets people know what God is thinking and doing.

Thus, when we want to tell others what we are thinking, we say it with words. There are other methods of communication such as books, but they are written words instead of spoken. Your friendly florist has a motto: "Say It With Flowers," but even this token is not a substitute for words on a long-term basis. We reveal what is in our hearts by our speech, for it is "out of the abundance of the heart the mouth speaketh" (Matt. 12:34). We can only conceal our true thoughts for a limited period of time then they come forth in words.

Since the heart of man is desperately wicked according to Jeremiah 17:9, that which comes out of the heart will reflect the true condition. Only the regenerated heart can bring forth pure words and thoughts. Nevertheless this changed heart continues to show marks of the old nature and can be a source of ill toward others. I think the most graphic illustration of what our words reveal of our thoughts is described in the writings of Luke in the sixth chapter, verse 45. Jesus tells us in this passage that a good heart brings forth that which is good; and an evil heart brings forth that which is evil: for that which fills the heart his mouth speaks forth. How can we say it any better than this? Utterances from the mouth are a revelation of the nature of the heart and its condition. As the term "heart" is used in the Scripture it speaks of the central part of man—his true nature, his likes and dislikes, and his moral and spiritual condition. What we are, we will say! Words reveal our innermost secret thoughts.

B. Words cause tensions and troubles (Prov. 26:20-28). A reading of the verse for this section of study confirms what we already know: "The words of a talebearer are as wounds" (v. 22). With our words we wound one another as we bear tales. Possibly this is the most repeated sin of Christians toward each other. It seems that few are free of talebearing and passing on to others unkind remarks and comments.

Often we cover our sin by what we term as the "spiritual approach." Rather than be an outright gossip we veil our rumors and idle tales in the form of prayer requests. The honest desire is not so much to pray as it is inability to suppress what we have just learned. We tell our friends to pray for a situation, then we enthusiastically reveal all the details that were formerly a secret. We rationalize this action by saying now we can pray more intelligently.

James is the one chosen of God to speak to us of the dangers of the tongue (James 3). He calls it "a little member . . . it defileth the whole body, and setteth on fire the course of nature; and it is set on fire of hell." This is a very vivid passage from the Spirit of God and should be read frequently by each child of God. We use our tongues to bless God and the same tongue to curse men who are made in the likeness of God.

Causing strife and trouble through the use of words is most effectively described in Proverbs 26:20: "Where no wood is, there the fire goeth out: so where there is no talebearer, the strife ceaseth." A fire will go out when you quit putting on more kindling wood; and, likewise, the fires of strife cease when a "rumor-rover" ceases to use words to fan the fires.

Can there be a more descriptive passage than Proverbs 30:33? When you churn milk you get butter, and when you wring or twist someone else's nose you make it bleed. So when you force wrath with words you have strife. Show me a church torn by strife, and I will show you a church where people are having big spiritual problems in their hearts.

C. Words feed our egos. There are different ways for words to wound us. Sometimes they appear as in the word of untrue rumors that do great harm to a person. This we have discussed, and the Bible uses the term "talebearer" to speak of this spiritual problem. There is another method by which we can be harmed by words. This is when someone may speak good of us and although it is not true, we want to believe it anyway. These words we call flattery, and the results are a puffed-up ego and pride. Such words can wound the person and destroy him as readily as untrue rumors. The major difference is that we make ourselves part of the destroying process by our own selfish desire.

Do you want the chapter and verse? "Faithful are the wounds of a friend; but the kisses of an enemy are deceitful" (Prov. 27:6). But even more vivid: "A lying tongue hateth those that are afflicted by it; and a flattering mouth worketh ruin" (Prov. 26:28). We like to hear words that make us feel more important than we are. But such words can feed our ego and the end result is pride. It takes only a minimal knowledge of the destructive power of pride to reveal that it will indeed result in ruin to us spiritually.

Words can wound us either by destroying us through the hatred of another person or by elevating us to a degree whereby we cannot be used of the Lord. All of this has to do with our relationship with others. Extreme care should be used to avoid wounding a fellow believer by the words we speak. Paul said it this way: "Thou shalt love thy neighbor as thyself. But if ye bite and devour one another, take heed that ye be not consumed one of another" (Gal. 5:14-15).

II. SMILES THAT HEAL

"A man that hath friends must shew himself friendly: and there is a friend that sticketh closer than a brother" (Prov. 18:24). This goes a long way towards saying that a smile from a friend often is the result of his friendly attitude towards others. It is best not to offend another, because once offended "a brother is harder to be won than a strong city: and their contentions are like the bars of a castle" (v. 19). So we want to deal with the second commandment as Jesus stated it: "thou shalt love thy neighbor as thyself" (Matt. 22:39).

A. A friend is a helper (Prov. 27:9-10). Sometimes believers have the feeling that they do not have a friend left in the world. This trap is of the devil and he uses it indiscriminately and frequently. Some of the great men of God have been ensnared in it. A prime example is Elijah. He had won a great battle for the Lord. The prophets of evil had been defeated on Mount Carmel, but wicked Queen Jezebel had set out in pursuit of the prophet of God. In discouragement and fear he ran. Alone, he then reminded God that he would like to die (see I Kings 19:4). His self-pity made him think he was the only one left to serve God. Elijah seems to be saying that if he were to die there would be no one left in all the world. There are times when we need a friend to help heal the wounds.

How thankful we are for the sweet counsel of a friend to help us through our times of trouble. The writer of Proverbs compares a friend's counsel to ointment and perfume that make the heart rejoice (27:9-10). The smile and a listening ear of a friend can make the heart happy once more. "Bear ye one another's burdens, and so fulfil the law of Christ," is the plea of Paul (Gal. 6:2).

What a contrast between the words that wound with a tongue set on fire of hell, and the words of a friend that desire to bear another's burdens. One speaks of a Christian who is not led of the Spirit of God and seeks to wound another. The other speaks of the ointment and the perfume of a friend with kind words of counsel. Such a friend can help a brother through any number of crises.

B. A cheerful heart is good medicine (Prov. 17:22). The shape is a circle; the color is yellow like the shining sun; the image is a smiling face. The popularity of this image is seen as it appears on everything from bumper stickers to pencil sharpeners. We call it a smiling face. The symbol makes good Christian theology, for the joy of the Lord should be etched on every Christian's face. The words "joy" and "rejoice" are often repeated in the New Testament. Peace is a fruit of the Spirit and it is an inward grace that makes the face to shine. Even Moses had a glowing countenance after he met God on the mountain. The face of a person who has met God ought to show a change (cf. Exod. 34:29-35).

The phrasing of the following proverb is so delightful: "A merry heart doeth good like medicine" (Prov. 17:22). Someone has added—"and it's an awful lot cheaper." True, it is! When the heart is happy we do not need quite as much medication. All of us are familiar with the fact that many of our illnesses are not due to organic causes at all. They are the results of our attitudes rather than the ills of the body. The second part of this proverb tells us something mankind is just now discovering—"A broken spirit drieth the bones." A person who always dwells on the negative aspects is a pessimistic person in all he does and thinks. However, it is foolish to attribute all ills to "a broken spirit." A broken arm is a broken arm despite any mental attitude you may have about it. Any amount of thinking will not replace a good cast. But the merry heart not only prevents many problems, it also helps to cure them.

Right thinking is a Biblical principle. We are told by Paul to "think on these things." What are these—things true, honest, just, pure, lovely, of good report, having virtue and praise (Phil. 4:8). So often we fill our minds and hearts with the very opposite of the above mentioned things. A merry heart cannot and will not result from improper thoughts and motives. We too often let the works of the flesh dominate our hearts—such as mentioned in Galatians 5:19-21.

A merry heart is a God-controlled heart that is filled with the Spirit of God. This type of heart will result in an individual having "inside happiness." It will also result in individuals making others happy as well. It is a two-way force, working both internally and externally. There are many medicines we use either internally or externally, but a merry heart works in both directions!

C. **Kind words are like honey (Prov. 16:24).** To complete our study on this topic, let us reemphasize the contrast between words that wound and words that build up or edify.

"Pleasant words are as an honeycomb, sweet to the soul, and health to the bones" (v. 24). In the Old Testament there is the frequent mention of honey. In Joshua 5:6 it refers to "a land that floweth with milk and honey," which presented a most positive mental picture to the Israelites. The Word of God is compared to the honey in the honeycomb. Honey has the imagery of the sweet and the good and of prosperity and well being.

Pleasant words from a friend are priceless. Is it not true we would walk across the street to talk to some people, and yet we might cross the street to avoid others? Some individuals give forth pleasant words, while others are always uttering words of gloom and sorrow that dry up the bones.

Pleasant words are like the honeycomb in two senses. They are sweet to the soul, which is certainly helpful to the inner man. We human beings really need strength in the inner man. The Bible encourages this. Sweet words are also health to the bones—the physical. This speaks of the same thing as the merry heart that makes us to be well in the body. A kind word from a kind friend can bring healing to the heart as well as healing to the bones and body.

REFLECTING—Words do wound, but a smile accompanied by pleasant words from a friend can heal. The kindest word from the kindest friend is the Word of God given to us from the greatest of Friends—Jesus Christ.

DISCUSSION QUESTIONS

1. Are you sinning when you discuss with others the problems of a third party?

2. How true is the old rhyme, "Sticks and stones may break my bones, but words will never hurt me"?

3. Must Christians agree on every matter concerning the work of the church and the Lord?

4. How does a "happy heart" work for the good of the individual? Would a psychologist agree with Solomon?

VI.

···

Six Things
God Hates –
No, Make It Seven

THE CHAPTER OUTLINED:

    I. A Look That Is Proud

    II. A Tongue That Lies

    III. Hands That Shed Blood

    IV. A Heart with Wicked Thoughts

    V. Feet That Run to Mischief

    VI. A Lying Witness

    VII. A Brother Who Spreads Discord

SUGGESTED BACKGROUND DEVOTIONAL READING

Monday—What Does God Hate? (Prov. 6:16-19)

Tuesday—The Prime Example of Pride (Isa. 14:12-18)

Wednesday—Christ's Dislike of Sin (John 2:12-17)

Thursday—The "None Righteous" Crowd (Rom. 3:9-23)

Friday—Beautiful Footprints (Rom. 10:15)

Saturday—Imaginations Need Control (II Cor. 10:1-7)

Sunday—A True Witness (John 8:12-20)

It comes as a surprise to many people to read in the Bible the words, "God hates." After all, we have been told He is a God of love and there is no sin in Him. This is correct, but the problem arises with our human acquaintance with hate. Our experience and definition of hate is all negative and wrong. We express very little righteous dislike for things which are harmful to good and right. A God who is righteous and sinless must be in opposition to that which is wrong and sinful. God must hate sin or He cannot be perfect and holy.

When we understand hate to mean "a strong aversion" or "to dislike exceedingly," we can understand why God hates sin. God's hate is not mixed with malice and enmity as is that of the fallen human race. Jesus, for example, disliked what He found in the Temple, and His righteous aversion to such conditions brought forth strong reactions in His perfect nature. He responded to the situation with immediate resistance and this was all within the limits of His perfect being.

Now what is God averse to and what does He hate with a righteous cause? The writer of the Book of Proverbs gives us some insight into actions in humans which God hates. The eyes, tongue, hands, heart and feet are used in acts to run contrary to the will of God. If you will compare the passage we are studying with Romans, chapter 3, you will find a striking parallel. Time and space will permit us to hit only the high spots of this area of study. Nevertheless, you will become aware that the things which God hates are very common practices of humanity. They are not far removed nor uncommon to any of us. The happy encouraging thought is that though God hates sin, His grace is sufficient to forgive the repentant sinner.

I.   A LOOK THAT IS PROUD (Prov. 6:17)

There is a good reason to start the list of abominations to God with "a proud look." This sin forms the foundation for unrighteousness in the Scriptures. It was probably the very first sin in the universe and was committed by one of the angels of God—Lucifer. Isaiah 14:12-18 gives us the account of the rebellion and disobedience of one who wanted to "be like the most High [God]." In fact, He wanted to be worshiped and to have the very place and position which God held. "I will" is repeated again and again. Pride is the elevation of self to a level that is neither justified nor deserved by a person. It is the basis for the list of things that God hates. Pride will prompt a person to go to all lengths to get things he desires. An angel became a devil when he permitted pride to govern his unholy desires. And today the supremacy of pride continues to destroy the lives of people in every walk of life.

Satan used the trap of pride on Adam and Eve. Eve heard the appeal of pride from the serpent in the Garden (cf. Gen. 3:4-6). He told her she would be wise and "ye shall be as gods, knowing good and evil." This was indeed an appeal to the first lady, and she responded. She sinned when she disobeyed God's clear command. But the channel the devil used to reach her was by tempting her with the prospect of being something that she was not. No wonder this worked so well—for Eve would certainly desire to be like God. A once-beautiful angel had coveted status and he now used similar bait to bring about the entrance of sin into the human race.

Is it a surprise that on the list of things God hates we find pride receives the number one place? Sin entered the universe by pride and the sin was committed by Eve. She yielded to the temptation which was based on pride. It is still very much with us and it continues to be harmful to many Christians. It also keeps many unbelievers away from God. They seemingly cannot give up their pride and admit they are sinners, even though this is a fundamental necessity. The admission of guilt must be followed by faith in the work of Christ on the cross.

II. A TONGUE THAT LIES (Prov. 6:17)

Number two on God's "hate list" is the tongue that lies.

This "hate" has close kinship with pride due to the purpose governing each of these sins. People lie to cover up their sins, but they also lie to make themselves appear to be better than they really are. Untruthfulness is diametrically opposed to the very nature of God. God is righteous and there is no untruth in Him; therefore, untruthfulness totally contradicts His nature. Jesus said, "I am the way, the truth, and the life" (John 14:6). When we lie we are responding to a situation in the opposite manner in which God would respond. So it is easy to see why He looks upon lying as a sin. Lying has as its intent to deceive and to mislead a person into accepting something that is not true. Call it a white lie or a black one! It all comes to the very same end—it is not truth, thus a lie.

While God is truth and is the source of truth, it is not difficult to discover the opposite. Jesus said of the devil, "a liar, and the father of it" (John 8:44). It is evident from this statement who is a liar and also who is the chief instigator of lies. Certainly the practice of falsifying does not come from God, but rather from the devil.

Let us look at two passages that dogmatically state God's position in relationship to lies. "It . . . [is] impossible for God to lie" (Heb. 6:18), and "in hope of eternal life, which God, that cannot lie, promised before the world began" (Titus 1:2). We have on one hand the father of lies—the devil, and on the other hand—truth and God. Here we are in the middle and who are we going to follow? Time after time the Scriptures tell us to abstain from untruth, and the commands are clear. Yet this world is filled with people who constantly practice this sin—and many of them are believers. We should learn the injunction of "Let your yea be yea; and your nay, nay." If we go against this principle, we find ourselves in opposition to God.

III. HANDS THAT SHED INNOCENT BLOOD (Prov. 6:17).

Again on the list of abominations unto God is the sin of

shedding innocent blood. This comes as a surprise to no one. A child in the primary department of the Sunday School who has been exposed to the Ten Commandments is aware of the truth "Thou shalt not kill" (Exod. 20:13). Man is created in the image and the likeness of God Himself. When life is taken in an act of murder, the highest order of God's creation has been sinned against. Murder is one of the most rapidly increasing crimes in America today. This is evident as we observe our larger cities recording hundreds of murders per year. In most of the cases the murderer is never brought to trial and if he is, seldom is he convicted of his crime. In the Old Testament God placed a very high penalty on taking of human life and the shedding of innocent blood. Government was granted the permission to take the life of the murderer. Many have declared this to be inhuman and cruel, and capital punishment is not popular in our courts of law today. We too often stress the rights of the guilty and forget the rights of the innocent. Read Genesis 9:6—this statement seems to be crystal clear in meaning.

Jesus, in His Sermon on the Mount, places a higher teaching on the matter of anger and our attitudes towards others. Matthew 5:21-22 not only speaks on the sin of killing, but also speaks of the sin of having anger in the heart towards others. He further states that "whosoever shall kill shall be in danger of the judgment." This crime against man and sin against God will not go unnoticed. Oftentimes we tend to think that just because our civil system relaxes its standards and changes the laws that things are different. Laws do not change with God, and those who think they have escaped punishment here will have quite a surprise when they stand at the judgment seat of Christ Jesus. God indeed hates murder and the shedding of innocent blood.

IV. HEARTS THAT DEVISE WICKED IMAGINATIONS (Prov. 6:18)

Throughout the Scriptures there are references to the fact

that imaginations of man are evil. The imagination seems to speak of the thoughts and desires of man. These thoughts and desires became the sinful purposes to which man spent his efforts. We will cite only a few of these incidents in the Bible that speak of evil imaginations. The flood of Noah's time was probably one of the most devastating works of judgment in the history of mankind. It compares only to the final judgment and the outpouring of God's wrath that is recorded in the Book of Revelation. Why did God bring a catastrophe on the earth such as the flood? It was because man revealed he was controlled by an evil nature—"every imagination of the thoughts of his heart was only evil continually" (Gen. 6:5). Again we note the heart is associated with the imaginations of man—his innermost desires and purposes. The word "heart" is used in the Scripture to designate the center of desires and affections. Our sinful acts begin with sinful desires in the heart. James speaks of this as a man being tempted when he is drawn away of his own lust and enticed. Lust then leads to sin and sin is completed in death (cf. James 1:14-16). So when God looked down on the world of Noah's time, He saw people who had turned from thoughts of God to imaginations that were evil continually. Judgment quickly followed because God hates wicked imaginations.

Paul gives us some specific instruction to help guard against the problem of this sin. He suggests a very positive action: "Casting down imaginations, and every high thing that exalteth itself against the knowledge of God, and bringing into captivity every thought to the obedience of Christ" (II Cor. 10:5). What a beautiful description of capturing our thoughts and imaginations, and not letting them run loose to cause trouble and to sin against God. The casting down of imaginations seems to speak of pulling something down and crushing it or destroying it so that no future use will be made of it. Unfortunately, too many people harbor and protect evil imaginations and nurture them until they become monsters that eventually destroy their victims. Fortunately, hearts that devise evil can be cured by God as we obey the instructions of the Bible.

V. FEET THAT ARE SWIFT IN RUNNING TO MISCHIEF (Prov. 6:18)

The feet are described as the least comely of our members. Yet they are also pictured in a much more positive light in the area of Christian living. In picturing the depravity of mankind Paul says of sinners, "Their feet are swift to shed blood" (Rom. 3:15). Now we all know feet do not shed blood, but they certainly can be the vehicle to transport someone to a place where the blood can be shed. We live in a society that has always been seeking means to speed up our means of travel. Our feet were not fast enough to get us around, so animals such as horses helped to take us off our feet. Then we turned to boats and trains and then came airplanes—who knows what is next! Daniel says in the end time we will be traveling to and fro on the earth at greater speeds (cf. Dan. 12:4). When the feet are used to convey a person to deeds of evil, it is noted that God is not pleased with this type of action.

However, let us note two positive examples of how the feet can be used for good and the will of God. The bearer of the message of Christ is described in Romans 10:15 as having beautiful feet because they are preaching "the gospel of peace." In Ephesians 6:15 we are encouraged to have our feet "shod with the preparation of the gospel of peace." In both passages Paul uses the very same phrase "the gospel of peace."

As is true in most cases we can take what we have and make a choice. We can use the members of our body to glorify God and obey Him, or we can break His commandments and sin by using those same members to bring the wrath and judgment of God to our lives.

VI. A FALSE WITNESS THAT SPEAKETH LIES (Prov. 6:19)

Is the writer of Proverbs repeating himself? Has he not just stated that God dislikes a lying tongue? Yes, but I think he is speaking of a more specific case in this statement. Notice it is a witness to whom he is making reference. A witness is a person whose duty and responsibility is to tell the truth. It is his sole purpose. As a witness comes to trial he is to relate what he *knows* to be true about a given situation. Jesus speaks of witnesses regarding His own person. The Pharisees called Him into account for being His own witness to His deity (John 8:13). His response was that God was also a witness to this fact and in the light of two witnesses and the law it was confirmed (cf. vv. 17-18).

Probably the most despicable of all false witnesses are those found in religious circles. The Old Testament speaks out firmly against them in many of the books of the prophets. For a New Testament reference I would suggest II Corinthians 11:13-14. The point remains the same in all illustrations. The person who is called upon to tell the truth as a witness and then lies is a person who is not found in the circle of God's favor.

VII. HE THAT SOWETH DISCORD AMONG THE BRETHREN (Prov. 6:19)

The list of six things that God hates is interesting in that there is an addition making a final total of seven. I would like to think the writer had not forgotten one, but used this form of writing to bring out a firm emphasis. We have spent some time on the use of the tongue and how it can divide and hurt people. Therefore, we will not dwell on this aspect of discord.

Here I would like to point out the reason the sower of discord is an abomination unto the Lord. The work of God has been on the behalf of uniting a fallen people. Sin caused the separation between God and man, and this continuing sin leads to all of the admonitions we have been dealing with in this passage. The First Epistle of John repeats a common theme—we cannot love God and hate our brothers. This is a completely incompatible action. Restoration to God through the new birth should bring with it a corresponding love relationship to other people for whom Christ died. We are saved and brought into the body of Christ, and it takes no great logic to figure out we are not to fight other members of the very same body. The price paid by God to accomplish the work of salvation should be a sufficient clue to the importance He placed upon it. It is an abomination to God to have a sower of discord in the ranks.

Could God hate such a circumstance? If hate means He has a strong aversion to it, the answer is YES! Many Christian people who consider themselves to be a separated people are no such thing. They are pious, religious people who are undoing the work of God, and He does not like what they are doing. Call a sower of discord by any other fancy name, it still comes back to the truth—it is still on God's most disliked list.

REFLECTING—Here we have studied a number of things for which God has an aversion and dislike because they are contrary to His will. They are in actuality a list of sins. God always hates sin.

DISCUSSION QUESTIONS

1. What does the word "hate" mean to you? Is it always wrong to hate?

2. Does God hate? What do you think of the following statement: "It is all right for God to hate, but it is wrong for man to hate"?

3. Since Scripture assigns wrong acts to parts of the body, are *they* responsible for these sins?

4. What motivates a person to sow discord among the brethren? What should our response be to such people?

VII.

Small, But Smart!

THE CHAPTER OUTLINED:

I. **A Wise Ant Always Prepares**
   - A. The Ant
   - B. The Limitations of an Ant
   - C. The Compensation of Wisdom
   - D. Application of the Proverb

II. **The Coneys Seek a Haven**
   - A. A Coney Is . . .
   - B. Coneys Have Limitations
   - C. Coneys Are Exceedingly Wise
   - D. Application of the Proverb

III. **The Locust Has Organization**
   - A. The Locust
   - B. Locusts Have Limitations
   - C. The Locusts Band Together
   - D. Application of the Proverb

IV. **The Spider or Lizard Has Persistence**
   - A. The Lizard
   - B. The Lizard's Limitations
   - C. The Lizard's Perseverance
   - D. Application of the Proverb

SUGGESTED DAILY DEVOTIONAL READING

Monday—Small But Smart (Prov. 30:24-28)

Tuesday—Weak But Chosen (I Cor. 1:26-31)

Wednesday—Planning in God's Will (James 4:13-17)

Thursday—A Shelter in the Time of Storm (Ps. 62:1-8)

Friday—Running Is Not Always Wrong (I Tim. 6:9-16)

Saturday—Persevering in Prayer (Matt. 7:7-12)

Sunday—Courage Will Not Be Discouraged (Heb. 12:1-4)

The Book of Proverbs is filled with small pockets of spiritual delights. In a devotional reading of the book they come as pleasant surprises to the mind and the heart. One of the great pities I have for many is that they do not delight in the little joys that result from observation. A lady once questioned me because of the exciting things that happened in my life. She said she had such a dull and dreary life. My answer to this is that life is literally filled with continuing incidents that can teach us thrilling and exciting lessons. Jesus used the illustrations of everyday life as a means of presenting great truths. In our present study we come to several humble illustrations that can teach us wisdom. The writer takes four different small animals or insects, shows their limitations, and then presents a solution to those limitations and calls the creatures "wise."

The lesson in all of this is that true wisdom is indicated by the ability to recognize one's problems and limitations and then to set about to compensate for them. There is no perfect person—morally, intellectually or physically. It is a sign of maturity when one accepts the knowledge of his abilities and disabilities. And it is the step of wisdom to know what to do about the existing condition. The ant, the coney, the locust, and the spider all have certain limitations, but in each case each one is portrayed as wise. There was a solution available to every crisis. May we be as wise as they.

In our study we will proceed in the following way: First we will identify the creature, then his limitation, followed by his specific act of wisdom. Our final step will be to illustrate and apply the evident truths to our lives as children of the Lord.

I. A WISE ANT ALWAYS PREPARES (Prov. 30:24-25)

A. The ant. As has been noted, the four creatures used as illustrations are all small. The ant certainly fits into this category. Every child has sat with utter fascination and watched ants at work. Their ability to carry huge loads has become legendary and their ability to find food is uncanny. Drop a piece of cookie or a piece of candy on a warm summer day. It is like a signal to all of the ants in the surrounding territory to come to the feast. They come in long lines with a mind singled to a definite purpose—to take advantage of an unexpected treat. We are aware of many different kinds of ants and their various sizes and colors. Some hibernate while others do not. In spite of the wide range of types of ants, we do not have any great problem in identifying this family of insects.

B. The limitations of an ant. The author says of them—"a people not strong." While they are able to carry loads in excess of their weight and size, they are not able to perform tasks equivalent to that of many larger creatures. The poor ant, hardly visible to the larger of the animals such as the elephant or the horse, is not a match and must be considered slight in size and of strength in comparison. I am impressed with the use of the word "people" when reference is made to the ant. This probably speaks of their organization and unity in function.

C. The compensation of wisdom. There may be nothing wrong with not being strong if you are aware of the fact. "Yet they prepare their meat in the summer" (30:25). They find a solution to their problem by their ability of foresight followed by preparation, and thus they are wise. In different countries ants respond to their needs in different ways. We are told in Europe the ants store grain, seeds and food stuffs—not to eat during the winter but rather for warmth and comfort. In other areas they store up grain for consumption when other food is not available. The point in each case is they are wise enough to get ready to meet the needs before the problems occur.

Why does such a small animal have such abilities? Any observer of nature must be impressed with how animals are granted different abilities in order to survive. It may be color to blend with surroundings; speed to outrun the enemy; a shell or covering for protection; strength to overpower the enemy; alertness for early warning—all are evident marks of meeting needs. God has endowed His creatures with the necessary means of surviving.

For the ant it is foresight—planning and working to get ready for a tomorrow.

D. Application of the proverb. The lesson from the ant is not hard to discover, and if the point may be missed in this proverb you cannot miss it in Proverbs 6:6-8. Here the ant is contrasted with the sluggard or the lazy one, and the sluggard comes out second best in the comparison. Our application on this point will be brief since we have already discussed this point of emphasis in an earlier chapter. If an ant is wise in foresight and preparation, it stands to reason those who take an opposite viewpoint are not wise.

So often an excuse is given by believers that the Lord will lead. I do not doubt His abilities to do so. But will He lead the lazy and the unprepared? Possibly by His grace He will, but I find limited assurance from the text of the Scriptures. The same God who can and does lead is also the same God who created man and gave him a mind and abilities. I doubt the Lord's continued blessing on the lazy Christian who will not exercise will or desire to look ahead and work toward a goal. Certainly, we are always to pray for the will of the Lord in all matters and we do not know what a day will bring forth (cf. James 4:13-17). Paul was unwaveringly pressing forward to accomplish God's work.

II. THE CONEYS SEEK A HAVEN (Prov. 30:26)

A. A Coney Is . . . . The word "coney" is not used frequently by most of us. There have been different identifications given to this little animal. Some have said it is a rabbit but the rabbit is not found in Palestine. One of the Hebrew words *shaphan* is best identified as the rock-badger which abounds in the Kedron area as well as the Dead Sea hills to the west. It has soft fur, brownish-grey in color, with long hair raising from the coat, a short tail and white on the stomach. It lives in companies choosing the cleft of the rocks as its home.

Coneys were very difficult to capture because they often would keep one of their company on lookout. A sound word of warning from the sentry, and they would head for the safety of the rocks.

B. Coneys have limitations. They "are but a feeble folk," says the writer of Proverbs. Such a beautiful description of their problem. They could not meet the enemy head-on and hope to win a battle. Such was not their forte or strength. The description of them seems to fit so well the little chipmunks who are possessed of the same problem. Little strength because of their size, hopeless indeed to meet the attacks of an enemy of any size. It is a delight to watch them move cautiously from place to place. Never getting themselves too far from a hole or a protective area lest they become victims of a larger and stronger predator. "A feeble folk" must learn soon of their limitations or else the time of learning becomes the end of the learning process.

C. Coneys are exceedingly wise. Do not despair for the coney or the rock-badger. What he lacks in strength he makes up for with wisdom. He is exceedingly wise. Here is another outstanding illustration of knowing what you do best. In this case it is running—running to a shelter where you cannot be reached, harmed or destroyed. The better part of valor is not to stand and fight when you do not have a chance for victory or survival. This the coney knows, so his first step is not to get too far removed from the rocky terrain that he knows so well. When he is here he is close to safety. The second precaution is to be alert to the enemy, that is why he has a sentry or lookout on duty at all times. The third important safeguard is to move when the danger gets near.

If you cannot fight them and do not feel it wise to join

them, be like the coney and get into the shelter.

D. Application of the proverb. Again the personal lesson should be an obvious one to the believer. I Corinthians 1:27 says: "and God hath chosen the weak things of the world to confound the things that are mighty." Here we fit the description of the "feeble folks" such as the coneys. We are not too strong of ourselves; in fact, the enemy is a great deal stronger than we are in our own strength. So we are going to have to be wise if we are not strong. This wisdom tells us to do three things just like the coney. First, stay on our own grounds, which we will call Bible grounds. This is the assigned territory of God's will for our lives. When we move into areas outside of the will and the grace of God, we are headed for problems. This is a strange and dangerous land.

Act two in our use of wisdom is to keep a sentry on guard at all times so the enemy is unable to catch us by surprise. How do you do that? By keeping your conscience and spiritual life alert and well disciplined. The Holy Spirit will act as your warning person. One who is sensitive to God and His will knows when the enemy is trying to gain admission. To ignore the warnings of the Bible and the Holy Spirit is certain disaster and spiritual harm to the child of God.

Point three in application is the warning that we must never be ashamed of running. This is a good spiritual principle to follow, if we are running in the right direction at the right time. Running from duty is failure, but running from a roaring lion leads to success. For proof of this truth let me direct you to a Scripture verse in I Timothy 6:11—"But thou, O man of God, *flee* these things . . . ." Specific sins and problems of the Christian life are to be left behind and lingering in the presence of these situations can only lead to danger and trouble. We are encouraged to resist the devil and his advances.

The coney went to a haven in his haste and for him this was found in the rocks. What a beautiful example for Christians as we are urged to flee to the rock of our salvation, Jesus Christ. In the Book of Psalms there is emphasis on the availability of a shelter from the enemy. To cite just one example look at Psalm 62:6-8. Here God is identified as the rock and shelter against the pressing problems that threaten His children. We sing about Jesus being a rock and shelter in the time of storm—what peace, what comfort! This truth has a strong Biblical background and foundation.

Small but smart, defenseless due to the lack of strength, but strong in wisdom. This is the lot of the rock-badger. How about us? Isn't there a lesson here if we will apply it?

III.   THE LOCUST HAS ORGANIZATION (Prov. 30:27)

A. The locust. High on my list of favorite animals or insects, the locust is conspicuous by its absence. My knowledge of the locust is limited from lack of personal experience. But all of my reactions are negative because of the devastation that can be wrought by these grasshoppers. They are able to take a field of growing crops and to strip it in a few hours. Traveling in great numbers they have been known to strip off all of the existing vegetation including the leaves from the trees. Their number is so great at times that they have been known to make the sunlight dim on the earth.

B. Locusts have limitations. The lack or limitation for the locust is that he has no king. It is a generally accepted principle that a leaderless group is not a particularly strong group. After all, organization by the means and efforts of a head, or leader, has been the order of events and has been accepted as a necessity. Yet here is an example, or rather, possibly an exception to the rule. The body has a head; a country has a ruler—a king or president; and business concerns have their general managers; however, here are the locusts and they survive and seem to do well . . . but there is no king to rule over them. What is the secret of their success and survival?

C. The locusts band together. As we have found in each of

77

the other two illustrations, the limitations have been over-come by the wisdom of the animals. The locusts compensate for their lack of leadership in a king by the means of banding together for strength. They do not seem to waste their time flying everywhere and opposing each other. They move in a group and seem to be motivated from an instinctive order whereby each locust subordinates his individuality to the group. We are told if the locusts come to a small stream, they will move into the stream in such numbers that they will fill it with a causeway of bodies that can be used by the others. Thus they move on into new fields in a solid grouping to devastate whatever is before them. All of this without ap-parent command and kingship. Yet success is insured by the strength of the total organization and not by the strength of one insect.

D. Application of organization. At first appearance this lesson of the locust seems to go in opposition to the principle of the headship of Christ. God, who as the leader, gives orders that are absolute and perfect. But a closer look will reveal another sound Biblical principle which is the banding together of the body of Christ. This is the strength that comes from unity and organization rather than everyone doing his own thing. In the cause of Jesus Christ it is the subordination of the individual's will to the whole of the organization that makes possible the victory. It is the personal sacrifice of each and all that leads to full unity of the body of Christ.

It is the harmony of the whole group in the church that makes possible spiritual progress and development. If each person must have his own way, then there is a constant con-flict with the others in the group. In the family there must be order and subjection to each other so that the unit or group may prosper.

IV. A SPIDER or LIZARD HAS PERSISTENCY (Prov. 30:28)

A. The lizard. We have a problem of identification at this point. Our Biblical translation leaves a little to be desired in two ways. The insect or the animal's true identity is not clear, and the fact that it appears he has no particular limitation is puzzling. It appears we are really talking about a small ground lizard at this point. If you have been in a climate that is warm you have seen the little lizard move about rapidly. He gets into some strange places—like in shoes or cups, pots and pans. In fact he will move into any convenient location—convenient to himself, that is. This lizard is even colored to fit his environment.

B. The lizard's limitations. His problem is he can be held in a person's hand. This particular desire is not one of mine, but it is possible to grasp him and he is almost defenseless except for his speed. Once captured he has had it. But it has been true of all the small objects we have been discussing—they are weak—the ant, the little coney, the locust, and now the lizard. Unappealing in appearance and undesirable for much ordinary value, the lizard seems to be a real reject in the world. But where does he turn up? . . . in kings' palaces.

C. The lizard's perseverance. Herein lies his ability to compensate for the weaknesses that he may possess. He is not easily discouraged—he just keeps at it. Possibly it would be easy for a human to get quite discouraged if he found himself in the position of a ground lizard. Unbecoming to the eye, uninvited, he invades the areas where he is not wanted--not an enviable performer is he? Perhaps you would expect the little ground lizard to be running away and to be left out of the good places of life. Surely it would be left to the more beautiful animals to live in a king's house. Possibly the king would have a beautiful horse, or dogs and cats of special species; but, no, it is the lizard who moves into the king's palace and there he makes his home. Why? Because he is persistent and ever persevering.

D. The lesson of the lizard. In the work of the Lord it is the principle of constant endeavoring and enduring that counts for much. The easily discouraged and the faint of heart just do not succeed. How many times do the Scriptures remind us "not to faint"? "Be not weary in well doing" is another admonition for us. Read Hebrews 12:1-4 for the prime example of what it means to keep going when the difficulties are the greatest. Romans 8 speaks of the suffering and the enduring that Christ experienced, and we are told that "If God be for us . . . [nothing] can be against us."

People with limited talents have been known to accomplish far more than those in possession of great abilities because they had the persistence to keep going when the others quit. Little lizards can teach us big lessons.

We may have spent considerable time talking about four small animals and insects but we hope they have taught us a lesson. The ant has foresight; the coney has a shelter; the locust has organization; and the lizard keeps at it. All are small in size and weak of body, but all are wise enough to find a compensating factor to make them reach their goals.

DISCUSSION QUESTIONS

1. A Christian says he trusts God for the future. An unbeliever says he never thinks about the future at all—he just lives one day at a time. Neither seem concerned about tomorrow; is there a difference between the Christian's attitude and the unbeliever's?

2. Are there times when it is wiser to run and hide than to stand and fight? Can you give any examples?

3. Why is unity and organization of the local church better than "everybody doing his own thing"?

4. Does persistence on our part sometimes indicate a lack of faith? Can persistence cause spiritual problems?

VIII.

A Father and
Son Chat

THE CHAPTER OUTLINED:

    I.   **A Father's Advice on Spiritual Matters**
        A.   Truth Is To Be Grasped
        B.   Truth Will Bear Fruit

   II.   **A Father's Advice on Making Friends**
        A.   Do Not Listen to the Sinful Friends
        B.   Do Not Walk with the Sinful Friend

  III.   **A Father's Advice in the Realm of Morality**
        A.   The Aggressive Attitude of a Temptress
        B.   A Temptress Wins
        C.   God's Attitude Towards This Sin

SUGGESTED BACKGROUND DEVOTIONAL READING

Monday—Family Christianity (Deut. 6:1-11)
Tuesday—The Dangers of Evil Friends (Prov. 1:10-19)
Wednesday—Walking in the Right Direction (Ps. 1)
Thursday—Discipline in the Home (Prov. 29:15-19)
Friday—Modesty of Apparel (I Peter 3:1-6)
Saturday—Thoughts on Pure Thoughts (Matt. 5:27-30)
Sunday—Child Training (Prov. 22:1-6)

How long has it been going on? I rather imagine it all started many, many years ago when Adam sought to give advice to his sons. As may be true in too many cases, the advice was not followed by both of Adam's sons. And the wilful disobedience of Cain ended in tragedy for all involved. The Word of God has encouraged fathers to pass on advice to their sons. There seems to be the ageless problem of the growing son looking at the father and saying: "Yes, but you lived in another generation. Things are different now." It is amazing how some problems never change. Why? Simply because the nature of man does not change. Truth, principles and morality find their origin in God, and He is not like the fickle society in which we live.

To show the timeless nature of this condition let us go back to Moses for just a few moments. After having recalled the commandments in chapter 5 of Deuteronomy, we read these words:

> Now these are the commandments, the statutes, and the judgments, which the Lord your God commanded to teach you, that ye might do them in the land whither ye go to possess it: That thou mightest fear the Lord thy God, to keep all his statutes and his commandments, which I command thee, thou and thy son, and thy son's son, all the days of thy life; and that thy days may be prolonged (Deut. 6:1-2).

Now note how the instructions were to be passed on in verse 7—"And thou shalt teach them diligently unto thy children, and shalt talk of them when thou sittest in thine house, and when thou walkest by the way, and when thou liest down, and when thou risest up."

In other words—morning, noon and night the children were to be reminded that there is one Lord and He is to be loved with heart, soul and might.

It has been said that truth is just one generation away from being lost. So father and son chats are of great importance.

We tend to think of them as discussions on moral issues. A discourse on the subject of the "birds and bees" is of the most famous variety. As we read and study the Book of Proverbs we will find information and instruction for both parent and child. We will find some basic moral truths and discover they are still very much up to date. One modern version of a father-son chat goes like this: Father—"Son, for some time I have wanted to talk to you concerning some problems about morality." Son—"Yes, father, what is it you would like to know?"

There are several chapters and numerous references that are pertinent to our subject; therefore, we will seek to bring some of them together under topical headings.

I. A FATHER'S ADVICE ON SPIRITUAL MATTERS (Prov. 7:1-4)

The first seven chapters of Proverbs begin with the words "My son" or some variation of these words. The words of wisdom speak to many different subjects. We select the opening words of chapter 7 because they parallel the instruction of Moses in Deuteronomy.

A. Truth is to be grasped (v. 1). The commandments are to be retained and valued. Notice the words of emphasis here are "keep" and "lay up." These words speak of an encouragement to a son to get a firm grasp on Biblical truth. It is the duty and privilege of the parent to see this is accomplished. I know it is impossible to force facts into a resistant body, but we are charged as believing fathers to take every possible opportunity to present exposure to truth. Too much of this authority and responsibility is delegated to others to perform. The Sunday School can help, the church will seek to do its part, and the Christian Day School will contribute. But, fathers, it is our prime responsibility to do this special God-given task.

In verse 3 a father is seeking to impress upon his son by

83

words that truth and wisdom should be written upon the tables of the heart and retained. The Psalmist said it this way: "Thy word have I hid in mine heart, that I might not sin against thee" (119:11). So we see it is the father's duty to expose truth to a son, but it becomes part of the son's responsibility before God to retain it.

B. Truth will bear fruit (22:6). It pays to give good advice, for it is a fruit-bearing experience. Many fathers and mothers have held close to the promise: "Train up a child in the way he should go: and when he is old, he will not depart from it" (Prov. 22:6). May we emphasize that training is not all talking. There must be a godly example set by the father for the son. A great deal of talk which lacks the "back up of living" will leave a son to wonder whether the discussions are for real. The father who insists a child go to Sunday School and then drops him or her at the church door while he leaves for the Sunday golf match is not what God has in mind here in the child-training process. If the truth is taught by word and deed, then there is a right to claim the promise. But do not spend the time fretting later and asking God what is wrong with your child if he is wandering in his walk when you did not do your part in the child training.

Another part of the spiritual advice comes in a different form of endeavor. This is teaching through the channel of discipline. Many modern-day educators will question the wisdom of Solomon in the matter of discipline. However, Solomon has equal rights to question the products of our educational system. For example: "The rod and reproof give wisdom: but a child left to himself bringeth his mother to shame" (Prov. 29:15). We are not discussing here the problem of a parent who takes out his or her frustrations upon a helpless child in the case of child abuse. We are discussing another form of child abuse and that is the permitting of the child to do as he or she pleases without any form of correction. A child is a very selfish individual with a fallen nature, and without correction he will become a selfish monster—not only in relation to his parents but to the society in which he lives. Our society is reaping the fruits of its permissiveness and it seems to be completely out of hand at the present time.

Godly training is probably the most valuable gift you will ever give to those who are yours. Spiritual instruction in both word and deed should be expected to bear rich fruit.

II. A FATHER'S ADVICE ON MAKING FRIENDS (Prov. 1:10-19)

What parents have not approached that delicate subject of seeking to keep their children from the wrong kind of friends? We question how to teach them from our own experience and thus help to protect them from the ones who would be of great hurt and harm to them. Such guidance takes the wisdom of the Lord.

A. Do not listen to the sinful friend (vv. 10-14). With a thought to the time the Book of Proverbs was written and then a look at the latest newspaper, one recognizes that times have not changed a great deal. These five verses warn against listening to evil friends, because their advice will lead the innocent into a trap of sin.

To be caught in the plot of a sinful friend is an intriguing one for the young person. The casting in of the lot with a group, being really "in" with the other people in your society—"let us be of one purse" (v. 14), is no small matter. No young person ever likes to be left out of the circle of friends. This is rejection, and no one especially desires to be rejected by his own peers—at least not without a cause. In these verses the father is seeking to give his son a reason to reject this temptation.

The son is offered material substance if he will respond to the invitation of these evil companions ("We shall find all precious substance, we shall fill our houses with spoil"—v. 13).

After all, what father gives an allowance to meet all the desires of an affluent society? Besides, it is for just one time and that will be it—or will it be?

Father is seeking to say to his son: "Do not listen!" A father knows the longer one listens to sinful friends and evil doers, the more likely he is to be persuaded. One of the ways to take the road to righteous living is to know when to stop listening to those who would lead in the wrong direction. The wrong direction is easily discovered. If it is not leading to God, it is leading in the wrong direction. So the advice is simple to give—do not consent to sinners. In fact, do not even listen to sinners.

B. Do not walk with sinful friends (vv. 15-19). If you *listen* long enough to the wrong advice the next move is to begin to *walk* in the wrong way. The reason the father gives advice for not walking in the pathway of evil is that the fundamental purposes are not right. Look at the list of the purposes of the sinners: ". . . their feet run to evil, and [they] make haste to shed blood" (v. 16). This is far from the purposes of the child of God and the will of a godly parent. It is a heartbreak to see a child running with those who are wrong. In this situation there is nothing but grief and sorrow to be visited upon such a union of persons. When God's child joins purposes with a friend who is not a believer, it forms a non-spiritual union. The warning of the Apostle Paul calls for separation from unbelievers (cf. II Cor. 6:14-18). What a powerful indictment of a false union with an infidel, since there is no possibility of a common purpose existing.

This application of not walking with the unbeliever goes into all areas of life. Many Christians have found difficulties arise through marriages with unbelievers; others have entered into business contracts and unions with the nonbeliever. Others have found sorrow by trying to keep up their contacts with sinners for reasons other than winning them to Christ. The stories all have a common conclusion, and it is a result of disobeying the clear revelation of the Scripture.

In concluding the discussion on a father warning his son about his friends, it will be well to read the first Psalm. You probably already know it by memory, but go back and read it again for emphasis.

III. A FATHER'S ADVICE IN THE REALM OF MORALITY (Prov. 7:5-27)

There are several extended discussions in the Book of Proverbs when the father seeks to warn the son against immoral conduct. We will look mainly at the portion in chapter 7. Both chapters 5 and 6 deal with this same subject. At this juncture in the study of Proverbs, it has become obvious that many of the admonitions have a common source. It is the Ten Commandments. Here in chapter 7 we have a broad descriptive passage that enlarges on the commandment, "Thou shalt not commit adultery" (Exod. 20:14). Let us, for the sake of easy study, divide this chapter in three parts. We will see the temptation by the adultress, the fall of the son, and the attitude of God towards this sin.

A. The aggressive attitude of the temptress (vv. 5-20). The father's advice to his son is aimed at keeping him from what is termed the "strange woman" (v. 5). She is one who is bent on immoral conduct and everything she does has this common goal as an end. She does not appear to be a harlot in that she is doing this for money, but seems rather to be one of an immoral nature. Her husband has left town to transact business elsewhere and she has been left alone (vv. 19-20). In her freedom from her husband's attention she desires to capture and lead into sin anyone she can find. She roams the street in the dress of a harlot so no one can miss her purpose and intent.

She is very aggressive in her conduct, and in this instance it is not the woman who needs protecting, as we sometimes think. It is rather the son who needs instruction against an apparent experienced woman. Her aggressiveness leads to her catching the young man and kissing him and telling of the sinful delights she would lead him into (vv. 13-18). Her very aggressive measures are described in such an expression as: "came I forth . . . diligently to seek thy face . . . I have found thee." In our present society there is an evident display of a much more aggressive nature in women than has been found in past generations. The casting off of modest apparel and moral conduct can be seen in immodesty of dress and aggressiveness of actions. In the New Testament there are instructions for the Christian woman so that she may present the appearance that is becoming to her character and her witness (cf. I Tim. 2:9-10).

It is an excellent idea for every daughter to be warned against the perils of immoral conduct and its consequences, but with the aggressiveness of the temptress in evidence the sons need advice as well.

B. The temptress wins (vv. 21-23). In the father's advice to a son he points out that the "simple," or a young man void of understanding, will succumb to her. This person is without understanding from several points of view. He is not wise as to what his conduct should be in such cases. He might be without understanding in the sense of knowledge. I rather think this is not the case here. This son is devoid of moral understanding which is the worst type of ignorance. He does not sense the danger and the end results of his conduct. This seems to be depicted in the description of him in the verses under consideration. Here he is described as "an ox goeth to the slaughter." What he seems to sense as a pleasant experience is actually his spiritual defeat and a sin in the sight of God. Just as an ox is led to be killed, the ox may not sense what is coming. He may think he is being led to a place of water or food. Instead, it ends in his death.

Another description is of the fool who is led to the stocks for correction (v. 22). His public punishment is displayed for everyone to see. Having committed the crime, he will now pay the price for the crime. Two other vivid descriptions are given as to the end result of this folly. One is of an arrow being shot through his liver which has very bitter results, and the other is a bird who is caught in the trap and the snare. When the temptress wins, the stranger loses in a big way.

C. God's attitude towards this sin (vv. 24-27). The father brings the matter to a conclusion as he trusts his son is getting the message—"Hearken unto me now therefore." Like all good lectures and sermons there comes a time for the conclusion and the summing up of the material presented. His description will all be in vain if the point is not made. The father's statements can be summed up easily. Stay away from the temptress because that path will lead to death and hell.

The words of the father are much like the words of Father-God. As we have seen, one of the commandments speaks out in condemning words against sexual immorality. The Scriptures are filled with warnings against it. It is not a popular warning because the cry of today is to do your own thing. Films, magazines and television expose young people to the matter of sex at a very early age. Permissiveness in this area is very frequent, and the standard of the day is shockingly low. Because the standard of the day is low does not mean that God has changed His standard to accommodate modern society. He remains the same.

Where does the house of the temptress lead? Note verse 27—"Her house is the way to hell, going down to the chambers of death." We all know that rejection of Christ as Saviour is the way people will be eternally lost, but we also know there are many things to distract from God and His will. This sin is one of the distractions. Why is God opposed to sin? Because His very nature is holy and He hates sin as we have already discussed in another one of these chapters.

By now you have become aware that the writer of Proverbs openly discusses immorality. Frequently there is a tendency to put it aside and act as if it were not there. It is real—and it will not go away. In conclusion—we must as parents face our responsibility and warn our children by word and deed of the awfulness of this sin.

REFLECTING—When a father chats with his son, he warns against bad friends, he encourages grasping truth, and tells him of the way of death in immoral conduct.

DISCUSSION QUESTIONS

1. Do principles of morality change with time? Are yesterday's wrongs sometimes right today?

2. Should a son always obey his father? What if the father is wrong? Who bears responsibility before God in these matters?

3. Since people—even Christians—are so easily influenced, what relationship should believers have with unbelievers? Complete separation?

4. How does a believer get the strength to hold to Christian standards when there is immorality all around him?

IX.

···

The Truly
Liberated Woman

THE CHAPTER OUTLINED:

I. **She Is Liberated in Her Social Life**
    A. She Has an Interest in Others
    B. She Has an Interest in Her Husband
    C. She Has an Interest in Her Children

II. **She Is Liberated in Her Business Life**
    A. She Is a Wise Businesswoman
    B. She Is a Person of Great Industry

III. **She Is Liberated Spiritually**
    A. The Fact of Sin's Bondage
    B. Truth Sets Free
    C. Salvation Is Freedom

SUGGESTED BACKGROUND DEVOTIONAL READING

Monday—The Virtuous Woman (Prov. 31:10-31)
Tuesday—Christ and the Church (Eph. 5:21-33)
Wednesday—Child-Father Relationship (Eph. 6:1-4)
Thursday—A Woman Won to Christ (Acts 16:10-15)
Friday—Freedom and Truth (John 8:25-36)
Saturday—The Truth Is a Person (John 14:1-6)
Sunday—The Power of the Gospel (I Cor. 1:12-18)

Moses walked on holy ground, and now I seek to walk on dangerous ground. Any free advice given by a man to a woman can be given only as a gracious suggestion. May I be a bit bold at this point and say my advice will be an honest attempt to point our attention to the instruction of the Scriptures. We are living in the days of "Women's Lib," and the term means a hundred different things to a hundred different persons. Thus, I will not seek to define nor delve into its full implications, nor will I seek to beleaguer it. Rather the approach will be a positive view of God's truth and recognition of His rich endowment to the world through His gift of women. Where actions in our society run contrary to the revelation of Scripture, there we must judge the actions to be wrong. When our pattern of behavior fits the Biblical standard, then let us be glad.

Let me also touch on another aspect at this point—liberty or freedom. These two words have taken such great abuse in our modern society it is difficult to find anyone with a proper definition of them. Generally speaking, freedom is taken as the privilege of a person to express himself as he pleases. This is not correct because such action would violate the freedom and liberty of another. Free people do not have the exclusive right to do as they desire, or else we would have chaos and no freedom at all. If a person were free to run around with a gun and shoot at whomever he pleased, then others would not be free to walk the streets or they would be killed by the supposed "free" man. You are not free to swing your arms about because your freedom ends where someone else's nose begins.

So it appears that what we are talking about when it comes to liberty and liberation these days is really a license or permit to exercise one's own sinful nature, and everyone else is to beware. To do one's own thing is another way of saying "authority be hanged." One is not free who is really in bondage to his own selfish will, and as we shall find later in bondage to sin.

Biblical freedom is the ability to move and exercise one's will within the prescribed limits of God's will. Political freedom is the ability to move within the defined limits of law with respect to others. Present-day ideas that defy law and authority are not so defined.

I. SHE IS LIBERATED IN HER SOCIAL LIFE (Prov. 31:10-31)

A. She has an interest in others (v. 20). The virtuous woman of Proverbs 31 is someone to behold in all of the numerous outlets of her life. We will find her interests center in her husband and children but they also reach beyond the confines of her home. She is one who cares for the needs of those who are less fortunate than herself. She senses the needs of other people and does something about them. Her hands are extended to the poor and the needy. One as busy as this person, however, is the one who is not too busy to have a heart of love. Those persons who seem to continually have needs of their own are generally not the ones who sense the heartbreak of another person. In your experience is there the kind woman who knew when to bake the cake or bring the little package of cookies. It was neither the cake nor the cookies that spelled comfort, it was the kind smile and the big heart. Here is a free person who is not in bondage to herself but rather liberated to serve others.

B. She has an interest in her husband (vv. 11-12, 23). Our liberated woman is married, but this does not seem to thwart her individuality as we shall later discover. She is indeed a person who is active and leads a meaningful life. Her husband's heart trusts in her, and "she will do him good and not evil all the days of her life." Our modern version of marriage has become a dim glow of the bright light that was intended by God. When marriage fits into His will and is followed in His way, it is quite an experience. Our virtuous woman wants to do her husband good and not evil. So she lives a life, not as a slave, but as one who is loved and who in turn gives her love to her husband. All the time he is trusting and believing in her that she will help and not harm him. In fact, she does so well at the task that her husband is well respected and is "known at the gates." A man of prominence and respect in the community is his lot in life. It is possible for a man to be a success in his chosen occupation without the full aid of a wise mate, but it is not probable that it will happen. The man who has matured to full measure of his potential has done so in all likelihood with a helpmeet at his side. One who compensates for his weaknesses and compliments him upon his strengths is his greatest human aid in life. By act of creation God made woman with her special abilities and emotions. Man and woman were never intended to compete against each other, but to complement each other in the physical, mental and emotional experiences of life. A review of the creation account will give us insight into the purpose which God intended at the beginning. This initial purpose has not changed through the years, but man's purpose has made a definite turnabout. The first couple was in a stage of spiritual innocence, but with the fall and rebellion confusion and conflict resulted. We will discuss this further under the thought of the liberation of woman spiritually.

But for now, it will be good to note the order which God instituted for man and woman. The Bible is very definite and explicit in the statements of this order. As we noted in the opening sentences of this chapter—liberty is to move in the limits of a society or a spiritual order. The woman has her greatest liberty when she moves within God's order. This is also true of a man or a child. Thus, it is not separating women for some special place of the unprivileged in the divine order. When there is the balance of position and surrender to the will of God by both man and wife (and shall we add children?), then there is the harmony which God intended. Man must assume his proper place with all of the love commanded. His is a role compared to that of Christ in relationship to the Church.

To grasp this order that results in liberty for all, read Ephesians 5:21-33.

1. *The proper order of authority.* Christ, man, woman and child is outlined in these verses as the line of authority. Christ is the head of the man, man is the head of the woman, and parents are the head of the family unit. This is not a dictatorial, heartless relationship between the parties, but rather a unit of society as God desires. Within this association is a built-in protection for the good and care of each. It seems to be formed on a pattern that has existed from the order of creation. I am conscious of outcries against what I have just said as I am aware of many of the statements against the Biblical order. But herein lies the heart of the present problem. People do not want to follow God's command. The man will not follow the command to love his wife as Christ loved the Church. This is indeed a very high standard to follow. Man will not always recognize that his wife is part of his own flesh (v. 29).

The order further breaks down when a wife will not accept the divine order of this social-religious unit ordained by God. The breakdown of the home is a spiritual problem and usually it is caused by a rebellion against authority. In this particular circumstance the rebellion is against the highest authority—God.

2. *A comparison of marriage to the Church.* One of the omitted points of the recognition of the family unit is the comparison given in Ephesians, chapter 5. Christ loved people so much He died to save humanity from their sins. Love and righteousness are the keys to His action. The Church is subject to Christ as He seeks to present a perfectly cleansed vessel to God. The parallel is that man is to love his wife with the same kind of love Christ manifests towards the Church. No woman ever need fear a position of unimportance if her

husband will follow this type of consideration. The liberated woman is free to move in the boundaries of the love in which she has found herself.

C. **She has an interest in her children (v. 28).** Her social life has been inspected from the relationship she bears to other people, to her husband, and now to her children. She is indeed liberated in her love for her children because she has expressed her love to them. "Her children arise up, and call her blessed"—kind words from your children are always sweet words. It is good to be praised by your friends and business associates, but the kindest of all words are the praise of one's own children. They are the ones who have spent days and years in close contact and have noted the flaws as well as the strengths of the mother. The woman who has done her task well now receives part of her reward for a job well done. "Her children call her blessed" can be another expression of her children "praising her." Motherhood has been minimized in the past few years and counted as one of the less desirable occupations. Children have been categorized as a burden that thwarts the personal wishes of a man and woman. This concept is not borne out in either experience or Scriptural instruction. A child's praise is a rich compensation for many hours of time and devotion and personal sacrifice on the part of the mother.

Before we leave this point, it has been the good experience of most children to know the love of a mother. God has placed in a woman an emotional capacity not known by most men. A woman has a tender touch that works miracles and casts out fears. Fathers can treat a scratched knee when a youngster falls from his tricycle, but the touch of the medicine and the application of a Band-Aid is more effective when the mother does it. The smile of assurance and the hug and kiss cannot be captured by any company that packages the medications. She shall be praised—our liberated woman. Liberated from self and lost in the ministry of love and compassion.

II. SHE IS LIBERATED IN HER BUSINESS LIFE (Prov. 31:13-22)

The "working wife" has been increasing in number in the United States for some time. The 1970 census figures reveal the following to be true: Married women ages 20-24, 47 percent are working; age group 25-34, 39 percent; age group 35-44, 47 percent. The young married and the third-mentioned group have identical percentages. As children move towards the college-age group, the necessity for extra employment for the mother seems to increase.

A. She is a wise businesswoman. A close reading of this section of Proverbs points out that the wisdom of finance is not the sole domain of the man. The woman buys and sells, makes good selections. She even buys a field and once she has the field she plants it for productive purposes. There seems to be no realm of the business world that is not open to her. She is not lazy, "rising also while it is yet night" (v. 15). She knows good merchandise from bad and will shop around to find the best.

Many other virtues of this woman can be noted and application can be made from the portion of Scripture. Search the Bible and see what you can find for yourself. The application which I wish to make is that many women are much better business persons than are men. It is a wise policy to recognize the individual talents in a family and exercise them. Often in the early days of marriage it becomes obvious one or the other of the parties can best handle the finances. This is fine, but both had better have knowledge of the state of finances or else there is trouble.

One problem of a working woman is that often her income grows larger than her husband's income. There is the potential of great danger here, first to his feeling of security as well as to her role as the major provider. Many marriages have had problems in this area.

B. **She is a person of great industry.** The reading of the passage leaves no doubt as to the extreme abilities of this person regardless of her sex. The question of the working woman in our society in the light of the role as a Christian has been much discussed. It cannot be argued but that a woman outside of the home is confronted with vexing problems and temptations. But it is also true that the nonworking wives are not freed from many similar problems.

The Scriptures repeat the activities of wives outside of the home setting without condemning them. The New Testament tells of a seller of purple who must have been a good business person. Her name was Lydia and you can find her story in the Book of Acts. Priscilla was a worker along with her husband, Acquila, and each had a role in the work of the Lord. The Bible does not stifle the individual talent of a woman if she has not moved outside of the area of God's will. Her talents can be used and developed to the full point of her potential.

III. SHE IS LIBERATED SPIRITUALLY (Prov. 31:30)

We come now to the greatest area of need for all people, both men and women. It is the person who is liberated from self and from sin who is the truly liberated person. In our world we hear the constant cry for freedom and civil rights and other expressions for self-liberty. Yet few would recognize the gift if it were placed before them. Since God is the creator and sin is the binder which tends to keep us from God, we are going to have to find the force that will break the chains of sin and restore man to the Creator.

A. **The fact of sin's bondage (Rom. 6:16-18).** Paul tells us in unmistakable terms that sin is one of the greatest binding influences in all the world. We literally enter into bondage when we yield to sin and its powers. There are many illustrations of bondage. Let me suggest a couple: There is slavery to a master, and/or bondage to a habit or an influence such as drugs or alcohol. In each case the person's will is in subjection to a given power. He cannot seem to break the influence and thus become free to do his own bidding.

After the fall of man in the Garden of Eden a number of serious consequences fell on both Adam and Eve. They were now to be dominated by sin and their own sinful natures. This was bondage of the most common but of the cruelest sort.

B. Truth sets free (John 8:32, 36). The setting of this statement in John is found as Jesus was discussing with the Pharisees His relationship to His Father. They could not accept His person nor His claims. The main claim was His deity and the fact that He could deliver them and others from their sins. He spoke of a faith that would bring freedom. Keep in mind the Pharisees were the religious leaders and such remarks were certainly an affront to them. But the point remains—Jesus spoke of freedom.

To be delivered from bondage is quite a promise. What was the truth that would set one free? In that Christ was God and His being lifted up in death (cf. v. 28), to be followed by the resurrection . . . this would be the greatest liberating power the world has ever seen. Good works, religious heritage, the will of man—not one of these could do it. It was to take the dynamite and power of the Gospel to set men free (I Cor. 1:18). This is the truth from The Truth (John 14:6).

C. Salvation is freedom (Eph. 2:8-9). The liberated woman (or man) is God's child, newborn and reborn by the grace of God and the shed blood of Jesus Christ. How this contrasts with the philosophy of doing your own thing and doing as you please! This freedom is the peace of heart that comes from knowing Christ has forgiven you and your sins have been buried in the depths of the sea, no longer to be held against you.

Christian liberty for a woman is the freedom to do God's will and not be hindered by bondage. No, no one is totally perfect, but, if one is in Christ, he will be looking forward to perfection, to the time when "Because the creature itself also shall be delivered from the bondage of corruption into the glorious liberty of the children of God" (Rom. 8:21).

Liberty is not an occasion for the flesh to do its thing. But as Peter says: "As free, and not using your liberty for a cloak of maliciousness, but as the servants of God."

Our truly liberated woman is clearly identified in Proverbs 31:30—". . . but a woman that feareth the Lord, she shall be praised." Her trust in God has set her free to be a person within the will and commands of the Lord. She knows not the bondage of guilt nor the fear of eternity without God, but she knows the blessedness of surrender to the truth.

REFLECTING—The truly liberated woman is free to exercise her love to help others as well as her husband and children. She finds freedom to move in various realms of activity, and her ultimate freedom is found in her Saviour.

DISCUSSION QUESTIONS

1. Does "women's lib" as it is popularly understood have any similarity to the liberation described in Proverbs 31?

2. What do we mean when we talk about liberty? How do *you* define liberty?

3. Why does God require order and authority as a part of His plan?

4. The Bible teaches that the truth sets us free. Is this freedom a complete freedom?

X

Running Rascals and Bold Lions . . . Guilt vs Righteousness

THE CHAPTER OUTLINED:

I. Running Rascals
   A. The Wicked Are the Disobedient
   B. Disobedience Will Bring Fear
   C. Examples of Fear in the Scripture

II. Bold Lions
   A. The Righteous Are God's Children
   B. God's Righteousness Brings Boldness
   C. Examples of Boldness in Righteousness

SUGGESTED BACKGROUND DEVOTIONAL READING

Monday—Guilt vs Righteousness (Prov. 28:1-7)
Tuesday—Fainthearted Fear (Lev. 26:36-37)
Wednesday—A Fearful Disciple (Matt. 26:69-75)
Thursday—Love Casts Out Fear (I John 4:11-21)
Friday—Reject Worry . . . Think and Pray (Phil. 4:6-13)
Saturday—Boldness Against Blasphemy (I Sam. 17:42-51)
Sunday—Faith, the Foundation (Heb. 11:1-6)

"The wicked flee when no man pursueth: but the righteous are bold as a lion" (Prov. 28:1).

Our topical study of this refreshing book brings us to a discussion of the inward attitudes of mankind. What we are will certainly reflect itself in our actions and attitudes. We come back to solid basics at this point. Every nation and people, every philosophy and religion have endorsed some form of opposites. It has been called light and darkness, black and white, right and wrong, but each of them pointed to a contrast of opinions and truths. The Bible calls it sin and righteousness, and all of mankind is in one group or the other. In the Biblical usage it is the contest between God and Satan, and which camp you are in depends upon either your rejection or acceptance of the person of God.

We will see in this study that what we believe, the truth we accept as basic, has a strong impact on our whole outlook on life. Those who are guilty and unrighteous are prone to fear and lack inward courage. The believer with commitment of body, soul and spirit to God is more likely to be a strong person and is compared to the lion—the symbol of courage and strength. These words of wisdom from Proverbs cut through the formality of our doctrinal terms and present a concept for daily living. What we are will be manifest in our deeds. The weak of heart are not likely to be the conquerors of circumstances. When we crumble emotionally or internally with fear, it will not be long until the body which houses such a spirit will also take physical flight. But when the heart is strong and fear has been replaced with trust in the living God, neither the spirit nor the body will turn in retreat. The attacker will soon find he has a very formidable opponent with which to contend. We will look at examples of both the fearful and the lion-hearted as we seek to note the practical differences between guilt and righteousness on the level of experiences.

I. RUNNING RASCALS

"The wicked flee when no man pursueth," so begins Proverbs 28:1. The wicked are the rascals, the offenders, the guilty before God and the reason they run or flee is because of what they are in the sight of God. There are other proverbs, not found in the Bible, that say much the same as does this one. An Oriental proverb says: "The leaf cracked, and your servant fled"—how about that to depict fear? One other Eastern proverb that would not be too acceptable in this day of Women's Liberation said: "Among ten men nine are women." We used to scorn fear in others by saying of them, "You are afraid of your own shadow." And so we could add to the list almost endlessly.

A. **The wicked are the disobedient (Ps. 53:1-6).** The first four verses of Psalm 53 tell us who are the disobedient. They are described as the foolish or the fools who proclaim with all boldness: "There is no God." They are further identified as those who do not have knowledge or understanding. This refers to knowledge of God's truth and understanding which certainly is not possessed by the wicked. The wicked are also described as having "gone back," "altogether become filthy," "none that doeth good, no not one" (v. 3). For a further look at who the wicked are, refer to Paul's statements in Romans 3:9-23. You will note the close parallel between these two Scriptures.

But the thrust of this passage in Psalms is in verse 5 where it is explained: "There were they in great fear, where no fear was." When God is rejected and there is no fear of God, such a one is open to another type of fear. This is the fear of where one will draw his strength.

B. **Disobedience will bring fear (Lev. 26:36-37).** When rebellion against the will of God is instituted, the results will be a fearful heart. This can be the result of a guilty conscience and an awareness of the fear of judgment. A stern warning is issued by God in the Book of Leviticus to the Children of Israel (cf. 26:36-37). God told these people when they disobeyed He would send a fainting to their hearts. They would be afraid of the driven leaf and run from the leaf like it was a threatening sword. With no one in pursuit the Israelites would fall over one another and have no power against the enemy. What a sad, yet almost humorous scene to see people running when there was no one around to chase them. This is what fear will do, and, yet, this fear was in their imaginations and not based in reality. But fear is like that. It is based on what is in us rather than what is around us. Most people worry about things that will never happen because they are living in the unreal world of fear and separation from God.

Saint Chrysostom, one of the ancient Church Fathers, spoke of the cowardice of sinners: "Such is the nature of sin, that it betrays while no one accuses; it makes the sinner a timid being, one that trembles at a sound; even as righteousness has a contrary effect. . . . How doth the wicked flee when no man pursueth? He hath that within which drives him on, an accuser in his own conscience, and this he carries about everywhere; and just as it would be impossible to flee from himself, so neither can he escape the persecutor within, but wherever he goeth he is scourged, and hath an incurable wound" (*Hom. in Stat.* viii 3, Oxford translation).

I do not know how better to explain the consequences of fear, because it does act as an external mirage and an internal accuser—all a result of sin and rebellion. It is a pitiless and merciless enemy bent on undoing its victim. To run from the imagined and nonexistent and still find no rest leaves the person to be pitied as he becomes a result of his own desires—sin.

C. **Examples of fear in the Scripture.** The number of illustrations will be limited because of the time and space. You will probably be able to think of others. We will list a few and give the locations of these events in the Bible. You may feel free to pursue in depth the ones which challenge you the most.

Abraham acted out of fear for his life when he lied and said Sarah was his sister and not his wife (cf. Gen. 12:10-20). The famine drove him to Egypt but fear drove him to lie.

Elijah's departure from the north country was prompted by fear. In this case it was the fear of Jezebel, the wicked queen of Israel. Elijah had won a great victory over the prophets of Baal. He had destroyed them and then the queen spoke and the prophet was headed out of town. In fact, he went all the way from the north to the south. See I Kings 19 for this account of fear and how it turned a strong prophet into one seeking refuge and safety in the desert.

The New Testament tells of a disciple who had vowed to follow his Lord to death if it were necessary. But Peter turned timid the night he betrayed Christ and three times this disciple claimed no knowledge of his Master. Fear seemed to be the power that closed his mouth to testimony and opened his lips to cursing (cf. Matt. 26:69-75).

No doubt you could literally multiply the number of cases in the Scripture where fear took hold of people. As a result of this, they wanted to run rather than stand for the cause of God. They do not stand alone in this type of problem for throughout the centuries others have followed their bad example and have fallen victims to the truth of the proverb we are now studying.

II. BOLD LIONS

The second part of our proverb is an exact opposite from the previous section. While fear will make a person flee when no one is chasing, a righteous person will become as bold in the cause of right as a lion.

It seems unnecessary to point to the lion as the accepted symbol of strength. The country of England long ago picked as its symbol—the lion. Many countries of Africa have also designated this same likeness as a sign for strength. Another ancient Church Father spoke of the power of the lion as it relates to this proverb. Gregory said: "The lion is not afraid in the onset of beasts, because he knows well that he is stronger than all of them. Whence the fearlessness of a righteous man is rightly compared to a lion, because, when he beholds any rising against him, he returns to the confidence of his mind, and knows that he overcomes all his adversaries because he loves him alone whom he cannot in any way lose against his will. For whoever seeks after outward things, which are taken from him even against his will, subjects himself of his own accord to outward fear. But unbroken virtue is the contempt of earthly desire, because the mind is both placed on high when it is raised above the meanest objects by the judgment of its hopes, and is the less affected by all adversities, the more safely it is fortified by being placed on things above." Certainly these truths couched in an ancient tongue are nonetheless true today than in the day they were spoken.

A. The righteous are God's children. Righteousness is not the works of humanity. ". . . all our righteousnesses are as filthy rags" (Isa. 64:6). Whatever we may attempt to do to find acceptance with God is doomed to failure, for we have no righteousness of our own. The only source of our righteousness is "through the faith of Christ" (Phil. 3:9). This righteousness must be declared to our account by an act of God. He alone has the possession of righteousness and the authority to impart it to those who meet His conditions. The conditions He requires are fulfilled in the person of Christ, His life, death and resurrection. This completed work of Christ makes it possible for man to be forgiven of his sins and be restored to the family of God.

When by faith and repentance we are born again spiritually, the finished work of Christ can now be put to our account. We are then declared to be righteous by a holy God.

No other decree is necessary but His and His alone. One of the clearest comparisons between man's righteousness and God's is found in Romans 10:1-10. Here Israel was by zeal seeking to be saved and with an ignorance of God's righteousness had set about to establish their own. Failure and frustration was the result. The law could not provide what they needed most. But faith in Jesus Christ can and does provide complete safety for the Christian. Here is a good time in this study to ask yourself the question: "In what am I basing my claim to righteousness—self or God?" If it is in self, then it will not succeed; if in God, I am safe!

B. God's righteousness brings boldness. We have identified the redeemed as those declared righteous and thus part of the spiritual family of God. We also know from our proverb that such are bold like lions. Some of the results of righteousness and justification by faith are outlined in Romans 5:1-5. They are:

> Peace with God
> Access into grace
> Rejoicing in hope
> Glory in tribulation
> Patience
> Experience
> Hope
> Not being ashamed

It is interesting that the first mentioned result of justification is peace with God. Here we are talking about an inward attitude in which the struggle between God and man is ended. This further results in the peace of God filling and flooding the person. When peace *with* God and the peace *of* God are possessed, the inward fears will certainly not find a place to take root.

We are talking here of our love to God and our faith in Him in the practical way. For we love God and we know God loves us, we are talking about the casting out of fear. This is

107

so beautifully described in I John 4:16-19. Let me quote a portion of this Scripture to emphasize this point: "Herein is our love made perfect, that we may have boldness in the day of judgment: because as he is, so are we in the world. There is no fear in love; but perfect love casteth out fear: because fear hath torment."

Note the appearance of the word "boldness." The bold lion is the one committed to God and His love serves as an instrument to destroy fear and cast it out. Anxiety, fear and worry—call it what you will, but they are all forms of spiritual destruction. "Be careful for nothing," just do not be anxious or worry, get rid of fear. How? By committing all to God, praying, and placing your thoughts on the right things, or should we say the righteous things (cf. Phil. 4:6-8).

The person who is right with God and has a clear conscience stands as the very opposite of the one who has gone against the will of God. One is strong internally; the other fears. Paul often spoke of the condition of the inward man as an important part of the Christian life. We tend to lay so much stress on the physical. Our prayer services are dominated with requests for our sick friends and relatives. There is nothing wrong with this, but where is the concern for the inward man of the same friends and relatives? It is strangely missing. When Paul prayed for the Ephesians his main desire was for what they were in their hearts and souls (cf. Eph. 3:14-16).

C. **Examples of boldness in righteousness.** It is a very easy task to point out the boldness of faith. The main problem is the time element. The Bible is literally filled with examples of men and women who lived with God and trusted Him—the result is "bold lions" of the faith.

David, the young man who could not bear the blasphemy of a giant, shows how courage and faith can overcome the physical weakness of a believer. Any child from the primary department can tell the story and maybe add a few interesting details of how David overcame unbelievable odds and became a hero of the faith (cf. I Sam. 17:20-58).

Jesus is the supreme example of righteousness and boldness because of who He is as the Son of God. His boldness at the temple in the early days of His public ministry clearly illustrates this fact (cf. John 2:18-25).

If you want a list of persons who were righteous and bold, go to the Hebrews 11 passage. Because of faith which opens the door to God's actions, these people were able to accomplish feats of faith that were otherwise impossible.

I believe the list of examples of those bold in God need not be extended. You can add your own favorites and see the point of this wise proverb—"The wicked flee when no man pursueth: but the righteous are bold as a lion."

DISCUSSION QUESTIONS

1. What is a "conscience"? Where does it come from? How reliable is it?

2. Do you think there is a worldwide consensus of right and wrong?

3. Why is there strength in right and fear in guilt?

4. Give a definition of righteousness. What is the difference between man's righteousness and God's righteousness?

XI.

....

Proverbs
Regarding
Life's Problems

THE CHAPTER OUTLINED:

    I. The Problem of Trials and Refining
   II. The Problem of Concealed Sin
  III. The Problem of an Unruly Spirit
  IV. The Problem of the Unsettled Home
   V. The Problem of an Uncertain Tomorrow
  VI. The Problem of Insufficient Funds

SUGGESTED DAILY DEVOTIONAL READING

Monday—Refined by Fire (I Peter 1:3-9)
Tuesday—Confession Means Cleansing (I John 1:1-10)
Wednesday—Swift, Slow, Slow! (James 1:17-22)
Thursday—Rebellious Sons Are a Worry (Prov. 19:23-29)
Friday—Bad Tempers Are Bad (Prov. 25:19-28)
Saturday—An Uncertain Tomorrow (James 4:13-17)
Sunday—Do Not Worry, God Will Provide (Matt. 6:24-34)

Did you ever have the feeling that everything happens to you? You look at others and you cannot see that they experience all of those frustrations that you seem to encounter every day. You ask your friend, "How are you?" He smiles and says that life is great, and down deep in your heart you respond with one of two possible conclusions. Either you envy him his lot in life or you doubt his integrity. Things must be going his way or he is not the most truthful person you have ever met.

But life, too often, is like one of Job's proverbs: "Yet man is born unto trouble, as the sparks fly upward" (Job 5:7). When the heat of the fire grows in intensity, the sparks are pulled uncontrollably upwards. So it is when you have fallen humanity—you irrevocably have problems. We live in a world where trouble and difficulties are impossible to escape. This should not necessarily bring gloom, because out of problems come the opportunities of life.

Because of sin the Saviour came bringing light and hope through His saving grace. As we review a few of the proverbs relating to the problems of life, as revealed by the ancient writer, you will see many circumstances have not changed a great deal. Yes, about three thousand years have passed but the problems remain similar. This may lead to small comfort on your part but it is a thought. Another, perhaps comforting, thought is that problems are not solely in your domain. You do not have them all, nor are you the first to suffer a new or different affliction. "There hath no temptation taken you but such as is common to man: but God is faithful, who will not suffer you to be tempted above that you are able; but will with the temptation also make a way of escape" (I Cor. 10:13).

That truth should be of comfort to every child of God. Remember, too, that others have also passed this way. But more important, God knows and He will permit the problems to go only as far as you will be able to bear them.

I. THE PROBLEM OF TRIALS AND REFINING (Prov. 17:3; 25:4)

Gold and silver only know purity because they are cleansed of their dross. The impurities must go, or the gold and silver will never know their true value. The first time I saw gold with all of its dross still clinging to it, I was surprised. I had only seen it in the more purified state. How do you clean up precious metals?—by the heat of refining. How does a diamond reach its highest state of beauty?—by cutting and by polishing.

So it is with the child of God. It is only as the impurities are removed that the image and spirit of God will come forth in glory. It is the abrasion of testing and trial that really brings us into full maturity. Peter spoke of this experience as "the trial of your faith" (I Peter 1:6-7). He termed it not in a negative sense but rather a positive one where its value to the believer was more precious than gold that perisheth. Certainly purifying brings heaviness for a short season, but when the testing has passed and we have responded to His will—then comes the end result. This end result is a better vessel, a purer vessel, and one to the praise of God.

All of God's people have walked through their days only to surprisingly find one day so different from all others. It started out the same but suddenly it changed. The loss of a loved one or an unforeseen accident, and then this day was different. The test has come and now it is time for us to react. Our true thoughts are revealed in the glare. Will we have the grace and faith to trust Him, or will we fall back to the old ways and thoughts? The heat has been applied—will it cause us to perish or will we become better people? Faith tells us "all things work together" (Rom. 8:28). Faith tells us "he goeth before them" (John 10:4). Yes, the trial of our faith is precious and it is also necessary. When we have suffered we can also comfort those who are now suffering (cf. II Cor. 1:3-7).

II. THE PROBLEM OF CONCEALED SIN (Prov. 28:13)

"He that covereth his sins shall not prosper: but whoso confesseth and forsaketh them shall have mercy." The question is not how to identify the sinner in our midst, for this truth says "whosoever," and that encompasses all. Only Jesus was free. The question is what will we as individuals do with our individual sins? The opening chapter of I John is a stern reminder that we only deceive ourselves when we say we have no sin. We camouflage our own sins but express mock horror at the sins of others while we, too, are guilty. The witness of the Scripture is clear and uncompromising—we all stand before God as fallen beings.

Our problem is . . . are we going to do something about our sins? No, not reforming and doing better. We have already found this is not enough. We need to be cleansed by the blood of Jesus Christ. We are told that if we hide the sin or attempt to cover it up, we shall not prosper. The good moral man can cloak himself in respectability and good deeds. But he will not make it, he will end up in hell.

To whom shall we confess? It is not enough to admit our sin to man. After all, man cannot save us. Sin is against God and it must be forgiven by God. I John 1:9 is a passage of Scripture that tells us to confess to God and in faithfulness He will forgive.

There is yet another aspect of confession. It has to do with forsaking. If you are truly repentant, you will desire to fulfill the requirement of forsaking the sin. To be sorry is not enough to fulfill God's demands. You can be sorry you were caught in a transgression and yet not be sorry to have performed the act. Paul cited the fact of the Macedonians' repentance as turning from idols to the living and true God (cf. I Thess. 1:9). There was proof of their repentance.

Those who follow through with this admonition obtain mercy from God. Mercy is kindness given to us by God even though we do not deserve it. Has it ever occurred to you how fortunate we are that God extends mercy so often instead of exercising justice towards us?

III. THE PROBLEM OF AN UNRULY SPIRIT (Prov. 25:28)

"He that hath no rule over his own spirit is like a city that is broken down, and without walls." There is a word to describe this condition—defenseless! In ancient times it was a necessity to have good strong walls around a city for without them the citizens had no defense against their enemies. What are we talking about here when we say a man does not have rule over his own spirit? Possibly a bad temper or an uncontrollable one would be the point we would make in our language.

An uncontrollable temper—now that is a problem! It is not an uncommon one either. A child throws a temper tantrum as an expression of desire to have his way, and that's that—there are no other choices. Everyone must give in to his wishes, or must they? The same child grows up to be an adult physically, and he continues to fight the society in which he lives. He must have his way and our temper-tantrum child has become a menace to others. He cannot be controlled at work or in the sidewalks of life. He gets what he wants or he takes it.

Yet this person who does not control his temper is to be pitied because he cannot defend himself or cope with the society in which he lives. Eventually he will be crushed by the very society that he hates and fights so against. If you have a bad temper it is a problem, and you must rule it through God's grace and teaching or it will dominate you.

Do you want to see the opposite of this problem in the Proverbs? "He that is slow to anger is better than the mighty; and he that ruleth his spirit than he that taketh a city" (Prov. 16:32). What a beautiful counterpart to our unruly man!

I have two suggestions at this point which make for good instruction when it comes to the curing of a bad temper. The first is in that practical book, James. "Be swift to hear, slow to speak, slow to wrath" (James 1:19). If you want a practical proverb . . . that is IT. The second suggestion is to read the list of the fruit of the spirit, and then let God have the privilege of making them flourish in you (cf. Gal. 5:22-23).

IV. PROBLEMS OF THE UNSETTLED HOME

The problems of the home are growing in our society and many are seeking a solution to the critical situation. We have discussed the role of the woman in society and her relationship to God. Here we would like to point out the three problem areas of the home—noting three people, their roles, and how certain proverbs emphasize the cause of the failures.

A. The problem of a father (Eph. 6:4). In the Book of Proverbs itself there are many illustrations of the failure of man as the husband of the house. He can neglect to provide for his dependents or he can fail to be a good moral example to those around him. Paul in Ephesians speaks of another problem area and this is the father who provokes his children to wrath. This can happen in many ways as the misconduct of the father leads his children away from the truth of God rather than to the paths of righteousness. The reaction in the child is negative because of the conduct of the parent. The latter part of verse 4 shows the positive aspect of Christian parenthood. "Bring them up in the nurture and admonition of the Lord" is the positive need of parents in their responsibility to their children.

B. The problem of a mother and wife (Prov. 21:9, 19). These verses have often been used in a humorous sense, but they are not very funny. "It is better to dwell in a corner of the housetop, than with a brawling woman in a wide house" (Prov. 21:9). In verse 19 we are advised that it is even better to be in the wilderness than to be "with a contentious and an angry woman." Just as a Christian woman, dedicated to the will of God, shall be called blessed by her children, it is also true a rebellious woman is difficult to live with—and so is such a man.

C. The problem of a rebellious son (Prov. 19:26). The third member of the household that can bring grief to a home is a rebellious child. He will be a shame and reproach to his parents. There is a growing lack of respect on the part of children in our society as the home breaks down. It is a joy for a parent to speak to others of the growth and accomplishments of a child, but it is a bitter experience to face one's friends with the knowledge of a breakdown in the lives of one's children.

A problem existed in ancient times when any member of the household failed to achieve his proper relationship with others of the family as well as with God. Time has not changed this basic.

V. THE PROBLEM OF AN UNCERTAIN TOMORROW (Prov. 27:1)

"Boast not thyself of tomorrow; for thou knowest not what a day may bring forth." James uses this proverb in his writings verifying the fact that the New Testament writers were affected by writings of the ancients. Truth is not the sole possession of any one, any time, or generation—it is ageless. Whether in Solomon's time or in the time of Christ there were uncertain tomorrows. And now several thousands years have passed, and we can all look at the truth of this statement and know its reality.

James expands on the truth of this uncertainty and brings several other points out for emphasis (cf. James 4:14-16). He describes life as a vapor that appears for a moment and then vanishes away to be gone from the realm of the physical. I remember standing before a window on a cold day. To keep myself amused I would breathe on the cold glass and the warmth of my breath would cause moisture to appear. As I withdrew and watched, the vapor would diminish and finally all disappear. In a short time there was no indication that it had ever been there. As a child the thought never occurred to me about death and dying. It seldom does to a child. Later in life the realization of the swift passing of time makes us realize we will not be here forever, nor will we be here very long.

James says this ought to affect our attitudes. We ought to take the Lord into consideration and say: "If the Lord will, we shall live, and do this, or that." A problem of life is to retain life, for death is so final to the physical. We are not able to plan and be certain that we have time to carry out all of those plans. It may be the Lord will see fit to end our journey before we thought He would. All plans must take into consideration His desires for us.

Keep in mind the imminent prospects of death and the uncertainty of our tomorrows. They are in His will. With this in mind it is possible to take the Christian attitude which is best described by Paul in Philippians 1:20-26. "To live is Christ, and to die is gain," but there is the need to continue in this life for the good of others. God takes into consideration the possibilities of all the needs, then in view of the divine wisdom He calls His own when He knows it is the best time. With the believer there are no unknown or uncertain tomorrows, all are in God's hands.

VI. THE PROBLEM OF INSUFFICIENT FUNDS

"For riches are not for ever: and doth the crown endure to every generation?" (Prov. 27:24).

"I do not want to be rich, all I want is enough to have anything I want." This was the statement of a lady who once explained to me her rejection of desiring to be rich. My only problem was I could not understand the difference between her desire and being rich. They both seemed the same to me!

In a world of inflation, deflation, riches and poverty it seems that no one ever gets enough of these material posses-

sions. Even in the wisdom of Solomon as stated in Ecclesiastes 5:10-11. "He that loveth silver shall not be satisfied
with silver; nor he that loveth abundance with increase: this
is vanity. When goods increase, they are increased that eat
them: and what good is there to the owners thereof, saving
the beholding of them with their eyes?" Can it be said with
more force than this? I think not!

There is never a time in life when it seems that the average
person will ever catch up with his wants. His needs, yes, but
the nature of man is always craving for more. Nevertheless,
the Christian nature can be different and it should be. An
awareness of God's Word should tell God's child several
things.

He can hear the words of a man content in Christ. A man
learning to get along with things and learning to get along
without things. The heart should be centered in the grace of
God and His will (cf. Phil. 4:11-12). Contentment is a rare
state existing in a restless and troubled world. However, it is
possible when the eyes are looking in the right direction.

Continuing our thoughts on the subject of enough and
God's will, notice the statements of Jesus Christ on the Sermon on the Mount (cf. Matt. 6:19-34). In this section of
Scripture there is enough material to cover hours of study
and some of the most practical teaching the world has ever
heard. To expound it here would be of little value compared
to what you can receive by taking the Bible and letting God
speak to you through His own words.

REFLECTING—The Bible is practical, just name the subject
and God has a principle or truth that will speak on the matter. Life is filled with problems, but God's Word is filled with
answers.

DISCUSSION QUESTIONS

1. What is the difference between a "trial" and a "test" in the Bible?

2. Is it possible to hide a sin so well that it will never be discovered?

3. If a person commits a sin repeatedly, is there any value in his repeated confession to God?

4. If a child is brought up under the teaching of the Word of God, can the parents be fully assured that he or she will remain in the faith?

5. Is it right for a Christian to go into debt? What about bankruptcy?

XII.

....

Social Problems
Are Always
with Us

THE CHAPTER OUTLINED:

I.   The Social Problem of Drinking

II.   The Social Problem of Temperance

III.   The Social Problem Is Really a Spiritual Problem

SUGGESTED BACKGROUND DEVOTIONAL READING

Monday—The Cycle of Nature (Eccles. 1:3-11)
Tuesday—The Folly of Drinking (Prov. 20:1-9)
Wednesday—Drinking Confuses the Minds of Kings (Prov. 31:1-6)
Thursday—A Clean Temple (I Cor. 6:15-20)
Friday—In Debt to a Lender (Prov. 22:1-8)
Saturday—In Debt to Love (Rom. 13:1-10)
Sunday—The Commandments Are Really One (Exod. 20:1-17)

Certain things never seem to change. This was an observation of the wise man Solomon in one of his writings. The opening verses of Ecclesiastes related the fact that nature gives us a picture of one generation coming while another is going; the sun rising and setting; the winds blowing as the rain falls; the rains rushing down the streams into the ocean, only to reach the heavens again. The circuit of God's law seems to go on and on. But notice the conclusion in Ecclesiastes 1:10: "Is there any thing whereof it may be said, See, this is new? it hath been already of old time, which was before us." This same conclusion may be drawn from our reading of the Book of Proverbs. The problems that confronted Solomon in the Proverbs are the same ones facing the 20th century Christians. So we can read the proverbs, note them, and abide by them and thus become wise persons. Truth does not face the difficulty of becoming obsolete. We will choose selections from the Proverbs that are as current as today's newspaper.

I. THE SOCIAL PROBLEM OF DRINKING

"Wine is a mocker, strong drink is raging: and whosoever is deceived thereby is not wise" (Prov. 20:1).

One of the great social problems of our day is drinking. It contributes to more problems than most of the other ills of our time. Presently there is a move to point out the ills of drinking. This campaign is not sponsored by the churches but rather by agencies of the government. It is an attempt to make people think of what is happening to them and those about them when they drink.

The cost of drinking is an enormous one. I do not refer to the price paid for the alcoholic beverages but to the cost in consequences. The high cost of broken homes and the extreme human suffering are examples. Death, so often, comes to the drinker as his or her body suffers under the influence, abuse and torment of alcohol. Another toll paid is on the highways where we are told that 50 percent of all accidents are caused by drunken drivers. This could mean about 25,000 people die from the results of these drivers, and literally hundreds of thousands will suffer some form of bodily injury each year. Add up the years and you will find that those who drive while under the influence of alcohol leave more victims dead and wounded than do the wars in which we have fought. You as a citizen help to pay the bills by increased insurance rates and hospital bills because of this one social problem. It is more than a social problem, it is a spiritual one because it involves disobedience to the stated truth of God's Word. This is sin! Note, Solomon tells us we are deceived when we drink wine and we are not wise.

"Who hath woe? who hath sorrow? who hath contentions? who hath babbling? who hath wounds without cause? who hath redness of eyes" (Prov. 23:29). What an interesting list of questions! I would suggest he who has all of the above symptoms indeed has a problem. The answer to all of these questions is: "They that tarry long at the wine" (v. 30). If you think you have problems now, if you were to become involved in strong drink, you would see only a multiplication of your problems. Strong wine when it is red will bite like a serpent and sting like an adder. The effects are profound and likely to be remembered for a long time. The only problem is that sometimes the victim never learns, and he says: "I will seek it yet again" (v. 35).

Possibly the threat of alcohol is greater than the threat of drugs to our young people and the rest of society. No, these things will not take them to hell, only rejection of the love of God will do that; but these evils will serve as barriers to keep people from the knowledge and grace of God that can and will save them.

There is one final reminder of the problems of drink in Proverbs 31:4-6. We are told it is not for kings or princes to drink because if they drink they will tend to forget the law and pervert judgment with their unbalanced thinking. I would like to send that message down to Washington, D.C., for thoughtful consideration. The reason: the rate of alcoholic consumption in Washington is probably the highest in the United States, and, though Washington does not have sole control of "fuzzy-thinking," it seems they are moving toward more than their fair share. I think because of the neglect of God's truth and flagrant disobedience to it, we as a nation are now suffering.

II. THE SOCIAL PROBLEM OF TEMPERANCE

The first thought of the average person is probably incorrect when the word "temperance" is used. His reaction would be that the subject of drinking is involved. Yes, this is one aspect of evident intemperance but not the only one. We will use the word to mean self-control in any or all areas of life. When we do not exercise self-control, we commit sin. Again, the tendency of people is to place sin as a gross transgression that only the "down and outer" would do. Yet, to indulge in intemperance in any realm of life is a temptation which must be guarded. We will look at just two in the Proverbs.

A. Intemperance with food (Prov. 23:1-3). To many we have "gone to meddling" when we begin on this proverb. Yet, the body is the temple of the Holy Spirit, and when we abuse it in any way we do ourselves and God a disservice. The proverb here is an interesting one and probably presents the strongest and most decisive diet ever suggested by man. "And put a knife to thy throat, if thou be a man given to appetite" (v. 2). That is indeed a rather drastic step to take to cure the problem, but a most effective and final one. We would not suggest that it be literally followed, but it does disclose the fact that the ancients were confronted with many of the same difficulties we have before us today. To misuse the "temple of the Holy Spirit" is wrong. This sin should not be committed by a Christian, not only from the spiritual aspect, but in view of the practical aspect of length of life and usefulness of the servant of God.

Let me branch out further at this point and propose that there are many habits which we pick up from our society that are not the best for us. The drug problem, remember, is a problem of drug abuse. For many of the drugs which find themselves used as channels of abuse are ones also prescribed by physicians for physical healing and relief. The problem is misuse and abuse. A Christian should be very careful not to begin to depend on drugs as a necessary part of his life. The need for constant use of tranquilizers just to be able to cope with life points to a problem. There are times when the physical condition of the individual demands such usage, but these prescribed drugs can become a crutch on which a person leans. If this situation occurs, one never learns to find the satisfactory solution to his problem. God has more of the answers than we are willing to believe. Why not turn to Him? Too often we hobble through life as emotional invalids and never reach maturity. This condition makes us unsatisfactory servants of God.

There are many other aspects of our lives that cause us trouble because of intemperance. Let us look at one more.

B. Intemperance with money (Prov. 22:7). In an earlier chapter we wrote briefly about money. Let us further expand this subject, thinking of the well-known fact that intemperance with money leads to the problem of overpowering debt. "The rich ruleth over the poor, and the borrower is servant to the lender" (22:7). The desire to have and to live like the Joneses has created spiritual problems for many Christian people. It is not an affliction of the young only, for many people have never learned to control themselves where money is involved. The present-day installment plan is not as "present day" as we might think. The concept of borrowing and lending goes back a long way in the history of humanity. Indebtedness can cut one's personal freedom and place him in bondage if care is not exercised. Solomon said: "The borrower is servant to the lender," and, believe me, here is a wise proverb. Many Christian people—pastor and parishioner—have learned the hard way that debt can thwart their testimony for God. Debt is an accepted way of life and rare is the person who does not have obligations and commitment to others. But intemperance concerning debt is when more obligations are assumed than can be met.

Perhaps we rationalize it is just another $10 per month on the installment loan to another party. Or, it is just another charge on the credit card to fill our wants—not our needs. Then comes the payoff and the unexpected financial obligation that we could not have foreseen. The "paper house" of finances begins to tumble and the lender must be faced. He is the fellow we talked to so boldly about his relationship to the Lord. Yes, we witnessed of the joys we received in the life with Christ and suggested our friend might have needs that could be met by the Lord. Now our witness is on the line because he heard us talk of the virtues to be found in God—truthfulness, honesty and dependability. You are now the servant of the lender, and the whole of your witness goes awash in intemperance about money.

"Owe no man any thing, but to love one another"—is the way Paul said it (Rom. 13:8). How many congregations have cleaned up the debts of the pastor who just left town? Men of the congregations have found it necessary to apologize to business firms for the man of God who was intemperant with his desires about money. When we have not met a promised pledge or obligation, we have not only sinned against the lender but we have sinned against our God. It is so easy to *talk* Christianity, but to live it is where the test comes. There are many churches and many Christians who lead defeated lives because they are not right regarding their business associations; consequently, they are also not right with God.

III. SOCIAL PROBLEMS ARE SPIRITUAL PROBLEMS

We have just given a sample of social problems and their

implications. We as evangelicals or fundamentalists—whichever term fits your personal liking—have a hang-up about the word "social." It is a word we seldom use because the association is not good to us. It is a community project which is not particularly spiritual or it is an activity sponsored by a liberal church. Thus, we keep our hands clean and our mouths closed in this area. The Old Testament prophets did not seem to have this difficulty at all. They were clear in their declarations and strong in their commitments. Please keep in mind it is God's Word that will speak to the needs of people. People must be cleaned up from the inside out and not the outside in. All of the soap in the world will not regenerate the world, only the blood of Jesus Christ can do that type of cleansing. But when the truth does come and the heart is made clean, the social fulfillments will follow.

What we call social problems really are everyday problems of living. This is where Christianity is put to the test regarding its reality in a person's life. It is not how long you can pray at a stretch that proves your spirituality any more than your ability to hold your breath under water proves you are a fish. What we can do with truth at work and play and worship is the final test.

Social problems are where we live, and it is interesting to see how much of the Bible is taken up with this very subject. There are long passages on doctrine and teachings as to the person of God. Long discussions can be made of what those passages mean. The doctrine will then form our spiritual foundation, but if you are the average person you must go out into the marketplace and live the life. How that regenerated heart and that enlightened mind will now function will be the determination of our spiritual success. Has our will been bent to His will? Has His desire become our desire? If the answer is yes, then we have made it; but if the answer is no, then something has broken down.

As a final set of thoughts on this subject, I would like to

127

take you to the commandments of God in Exodus 20. The Bible makes it clear that the law cannot save a person (cf. Rom. 3:20 and Gal. 2:16-21). This is not to be disputed as it is the righteousness that comes by faith that saves a sinner. Nevertheless, God gave the law for a reason, and that reason was to show mankind their failures, to reveal sin, because in failing to keep the law their transgressions are made clear.

It may be said that much of the law has to do with what we call social problems. The point I am seeking to make here is that our treatment of others reveals a great deal about our relationship to God. John tells us that how we treat others is a clear reflection of our spiritual condition with God (cf. I John 1:5-10). If we hate man, it is impossible to be in love with God at the same time. The commandments deal with our treatment of others in honoring parents, not killing, not stealing, not bearing false witness, and not coveting our neighbors' possessions (cf. Exod. 20:1-17). Social problems are not merely what we do to or with one another, they are rather what God tells us to do and whether or not we follow His leadership. We sin when we lie, because we not only harm the person lied to, but because God told us not to do it in the first place. Sin is disobeying God's commandment and instruction.

James bears down on this subject harder than possibly any other of the writers of the Scripture. In fact, his statements about faith working is so strong people have said he was a little mixed up on the subject. If you want a lesson on practical Christianity and how faith works in practice, here is the book for you.

Yes, social problems are always with us because people created in the image of God are always with us. These people are fallen and their natures are alienated from Him. But thank God for His salvation and a restoration of the image. Our treatment of ourselves and others will be the living proof of the reality of our doctrinal statement.

DISCUSSION QUESTIONS

1. Since wine is often condemned in the Bible, how do you view such passages as Christ at Cana (John 2:1-11) and Paul's instruction to Timothy to take "a little wine for thy stomach's sake" (I Tim. 5:23)?

2. The Book of Proverbs warns against intemperance in all areas of life. How does this apply to the Christian with an overeating problem?

3. Can we separate social problems from spiritual problems?

4. Did the Old Testament prophets place more emphasis on social action than does the New Testament?

XIII.

....

In Conclusion

THE CHAPTER OUTLINED:

I.   Knowledge Is Not Enough

II. Man Must Permit Truth To Take Hold

III. The Holy Spirit Is the Convincer of —
   A. The Fact of Sin
   B. The Fact of Righteousness
   C. The Fact of Judgment

IV. Final Statement of a Reason for This Study

SUGGESTED BACKGROUND DEVOTIONAL READING

Monday—Living, Walking Epistles (II Cor. 3:1-6)

Tuesday—Hard Hearts Reject God (Ps. 95:6-11)

Wednesday—Man, Created in God's Image (Gen. 1:26-31)

Thursday—God Brings Light to Dark Hearts (II Cor. 4:1-7)

Friday—The Holy Spirit, God's Illuminator (John 16:7-16)

Saturday—All Truth for All Needs (II Peter 1:1-4)

Sunday—Power To Meet All Problems (Eph. 1:15-23)

We come to our final discussion in this study of the Book of Proverbs. We have touched upon a wide variety of topics. I trust this has stimulated your thinking and opened a new area of study for you. And I hope it has started a love affair between you and the Proverbs. If we have succeeded in even a small measure to get you and these wise words in better relationship, then it has all been a success. Just a brief review—we have touched on the following subjects:

The Background and Purpose of Proverbs
The Fact of Knowledge and Its Basic Need
Wisdom, the Practical Use of Knowledge
Employment, Earnings and What to Do with Money
Words That Hurt Others and Attitudes That Help Others
Animals That Are Weak but Wise—They Survive
Attitudes That God Does Not Like
A Father Warns His Son Against Coming Temptations
What Makes a Woman Free
Fear Is a Result of Guilt; Boldness Comes from a Righteous Heart
The Home, a Cornerstone of Society
Problems with People? They Will Be Here for Awhile

A close inspection will reveal that these topics touch on just about every problem you must face in daily life. There is strong trustworthy advice for everyone in the Book of Proverbs.

The final chapter is intended to be a conclusion. It will be a drawing together of all of the above mentioned situations in order to tie up the loose ends. To touch on all the subjects in this great book is almost impossible. It is equally as difficult to have an outline for it. The intertwining of diverse topics is so common that it soon appears to be a patchwork of truths with distinct messages. Just as a number of trees make up a woods or forest, so do the proverbs make up a message. You can inspect each tree of the woods as a separate unit. Here is an oak, a pine, a poplar, a maple or a dogwood—each with a unique existence. Move back from the trees several hundred yards and then you see a cluster, a unit—the woods. Walk through the Book of Proverbs mentally and here is truth about knowledge, wisdom, morals, attitudes toward others, fear, guilt, and the family. Take some mental steps away from the Book of Proverbs and then think back. What do you see? Truth about life—how to live it and find success with God and man. Proverbs is all about Monday through Saturday living. It takes you away from the stained glass windows, the robed choirs, and the Sunday-go-to-meeting clothes and leads you into the marketplace where most of us spend our time. But when Proverbs leads you there, it goes with you offering excellent advice and words of wisdom about God and man.

We have walked through this book and now where are we? Would you give me the final courtesy of listening to some final conclusions?

I. KNOWLEDGE IS NOT ENOUGH (II Cor. 3:1-18; Prov. 21:29; 28:14)

We have made a strong point of the fact that knowledge is the firm foundation. Let me reemphasize this point so there will be no misunderstanding. God has chosen to make His truth clear to the world. The channel of revelation has been in nature, in written form—His Word and through His Son, Jesus. Without this revelation from God which comes to us through our mental and spiritual faculties it is impossible to know God. Facts, truths, revelation—call them what you will—they are God's means of making man aware of what God is saying to us. Wrong knowledge will destroy and lead in the wrong direction, and the wrong direction will result in spiritual and eternal destruction. After all, man's ways are not God's ways (cf. Isa. 55:8).

But it is possible to have truth and Biblical knowledge and still not have the soul saved or the individual walking in proper relationship with God. The letter can kill (cf. II Cor. 3:6-16). The law had a purpose; it was to instruct and make clear. There was nothing wrong with the law. It was the attitude of the people towards the law that caused difficulties. Even the truth in the form of knowledge is not enough to save a person. Though knowledge is necessary, it is not sufficient in itself. If it were, every person who hears would be saved, and we know this is not true.

In fact, as knowledge repeatedly descends upon people and is rejected, it becomes much like the rain falling on the ground. It can harden rather than soften. This illustration from the ministry of Christ referred to this very incident (cf. Matt. 13:18-30). Other illustrations of truth hardening is found in the ancient history when Moses approached Pharaoh with the truth of God. Pharaoh hardened his heart to the truth and would not submit to God's will (Exod. 8:15, 32; 9:34). There was nothing wrong with the truth. The problem was in Pharaoh's heart.

Further proof of this problem can be seen in other Scripture passages. Israel was warned not to harden their hearts against God (cf. Deut. 15:7); another warning (cf. Ps. 95:8); New Testament warnings (cf. John 12:40 and Acts 19:9).

Hardness of the heart comes from a rejection of the revelation of God's will. It comes when truth is not permitted to enter the heart.

What are man's methods of rejection?

II. MAN MUST PERMIT TRUTH TO TAKE HOLD

When God created man it was indeed a great miracle and masterpiece. "In the image of God created he him" (Gen. 1:27). Man had a free will to exercise as he saw fit. But man was also a moral creature with the ability to know right from wrong regarding the instructions as they came from God. We have learned from the material in this chapter that God furnishes the knowledge, but it is up to man to respond positively to this truth. Obedience is the path of blessing; rejection is the pathway of sin and sorrow. Mankind, by free will, rebelled and disobeyed God. The curse came because of this disobedience. When we have stated that knowledge is not enough, we intend to communicate the fact that salvation must be received by a person as an act of his free will. If he rejects it, this does not take away from the truth in any way, but it does take away the possibility of eternal life with God.

Man has a mind with which he thinks; he also has emotions and feelings, but he must exercise his will or volition and commit this to God in order for salvation to reach him. One of the major problems we must face as servants and workers for God is to keep in mind this volition or will must be touched. Our churches are filled with people who have knowledge but of these there is an amazing number who have rebellious wills and are not submissive to God. This vast amount of knowledge, not yet translated to wisdom, is—or should be—a great area of concern for those who want people to move forward for God.

The devil blinds the minds of people so they will not be able to know the truth of the Gospel (cf. II Cor. 4:3-4). If the person does accept Christ as Saviour, this does not mean the work of the deceiver is finished. He does not quit at one defeat; he will seek to hinder the believer, keeping him from maturity in Christ.

How can this problem of knowledge and will be solved?

III. THE HOLY SPIRIT IS THE CONVINCER (John 16:7-11)

It is the role of the Christian to be a witness, but the Word of God makes clear it is the Holy Spirit that must speak and convict people. Unless this conviction takes place there will be no motivation to respond to knowledge and truth. The Holy Spirit works in three areas of truth concerning knowledge. These three facts are basic to motivating people to salvation and Christian activity. If these three facts were not true, then there would be no need to respond to the message of God.

A. The fact of sin (John 16:9). If there is no sin, there is no need of a Saviour. This seems to be so elementary that it need not be stated. If Adam and Eve and the whole human race had not disobeyed God there would be no need for us to look to the shed blood of Jesus. But as this passage tells us, the sin is the rejection of Jesus, failure to believe in Him. A rejection of God's Son is a rejection of God, the Father.

People must face this fact—all are sinners (cf. Rom. 3:23). It is easy to convince people that they should be better than they are at the present time and they will even work at improving. This is called reformation—to do better than we did formerly. But to convince people they are unregenerate sinners is something else. A sinner is another fellow, not me! He is the drunkard, the fellow who lives in the slum and does not love his wife or children. So runs the line of the nice guy next door who only takes an occasional drink.

The Holy Spirit says the vile sinner is the person who does not believe in Jesus or God. And we can only believe in God through Jesus Christ. There is no other way to the Father but through the Son (cf. John 14:6). So the first fact needed to motivate people to God is the work of the Holy Spirit who teaches them of the existence of sin.

B. The fact of righteousness (John 16:10). If there is sin, and only sin, why worry about it? But there is an opposite of sin and that is righteousness. We have spoken of the righteousness of man and the righteousness of God in a former chapter. It is an actual fact that God's righteousness is really an extension of His own being. He is perfect and holy and always right. He is ever ready to impute this righteousness to the account of the person who will become a believer by faith. So God is righteous and His righteousness is available to all humanity.

Do you need proof of this? Jesus said the proof of the existence of His righteousness was the fact that He would be received back to heaven by His Father and they (the disciples) would see Him no more. What kind of proof or argument is this? Simply stated—Christ claimed to be God and to be equal with the Father (John 10:27-30). If He was not as He claimed to be, the Father would not have received Him into heaven. Jesus fully performed the will of His Father and is all righteousness.

Now we know there is wrong and wrong is sin. And there is also right and God is all righteousness. Man is a sinner but he has the possibility of becoming righteous. The question is why should man choose God's righteousness over his own sinfulness? A good question and a question that needs to be answered by everyone.

C. The fact of judgment (John 16:11). Here is the clincher to the whole set of facts. The reason to accept God's righteousness over sin is because sin will be judged as will the sinner. The high price of judgment is the eternal separation of the person from God. This is revealed in many passages of the Scripture, but the most dramatic is Revelation 20:11-15. In five short verses you have a judgment scene, and all who reject God's love are sentenced for eternity, to the lake of fire which is the second death. When the Spirit of God has convicted a person of sin and shown him the results of sin, this should be sufficient motivation to cause one to turn by faith to Christ.

There may be one last question by the sinner which could be: "How do I know there will be a judgment?" A good question, and again one that Christ Himself answers by saying: "Of judgment, because the prince of this world is judged" (v. 11). "The prince of this world" is an obvious reference to Satan. If this rebel would not have been judged, then there might be some hope for the freedom of his followers. But no, at the Cross, Christ in His death, brought to nought the works of the devil. Satan has been judged and so will all of his followers (I John 3:8).

Thus, three facts leave us with the necessary motivation for righteousness. Unless the Holy Spirit does His work there is no hope for man to find God. Our dependence on God is twofold: first, for revealing truth, and then letting truth work in our lives. Man must permit this truth to take hold of his life as he willingly yields to it. But man will not yield until he is convinced this is the best for him; only the Spirit of God can accomplish this.

IV. FINAL STATEMENT OF A REASON FOR THIS STUDY

This sounds like a conclusion to the conclusion, but I hesitate to finish until I reemphasize my purpose in sitting down to write this study guide. I have a personal conviction that the Church of Jesus Christ is failing to meet even a very small part of its potential. I stand at times overwhelmed by the reservoir of truth given to us of God. It contains absolutely everything necessary for life and godliness (II Peter 1:2-4). The power of the Holy Spirit that brought Jesus from the dead is within us (Eph. 1:19-23). And yet the Church (the body of believers) remains a powerless force in a vast harvest field. The individual parts of the church do not have sufficient impact upon the lives surrounding it. What is the problem?

May I humbly suggest one such problem? Is it because we have not yet learned to use truth properly? The truth is stored in a neat systematic theology in our heads. The files are neat and the reasons and proof texts are uncluttered. Step one is in order, and we could give a reason for the hope that is within us (I Peter 3:15). Step two is the problem. The truth doesn't seem to make it to our hearts and emotions and the center of our will and desires. Even though we are saved, we are still resisting truth and knowledge.

If there is one thing that Proverbs makes a strong plea for, it is that the wise man is the one who puts truth into action. The truth fits in the home, the factory, the office, and school. Wisdom works wherever it goes. It is Christianity, not only as factual data, but rather it is faith as a working principle. How we need this in our society today! Regenerated, practical people who are kind of word, true with tongue, compassionate to others, in love with God, and looking forward to heaven.

The world of unsaved people is hungering for this type of Christianity. It was the type of message Christ brought to the world 20 centuries ago. It was the type of Christianity Paul pleaded for in II Corinthians 3:1-6. To be living epistles and letters, to be known and read of all men.

If Proverbs has made you aware of this type of Christianity, then our study together has been a success and to the glory of God.

DISCUSSION QUESTIONS

1. Why is it that a person can have a great knowledge and education and still fail?

2. Should education and training in present-day society be based on Biblical principles? Why or why not?

3. Where does your responsibility as a witness end and the Holy Spirit's power to work in the heart begin?

4. Why do Christians often lack spiritual power when they are offered so much?